THE JONES FILES

BOOK THREE: JONES

A. C. JONES

ISBN 978-1-950818-98-3 (paperback)
ISBN 978-1-950818-91-4 (digital)

Copyright © 2020 by A. C. Jones

All rights reserved. No part of this publication may be reproduced, distributed, or transmitted in any form or by any means, including photocopying, recording, or other electronic or mechanical methods without the prior written permission of the publisher. For permission requests, solicit the publisher via the address below.

Rushmore Press LLC
1 800 460 9188
www.rushmorepress.com

Printed in the United States of America

CHAPTER 1

The Rosemarie is one of Roses newest container ships. She is at a huge facility in China being loaded down with thousands of containers. The Captain is on the bridge speaking with a small man obviously Chinese. Mr. Woo is secretive and ushers Captain Smith into the captain's day cabin. He closes the door and speaks in a barely audible voice. He offers the captain a brown envelope stuffed with American currency. The bills are not new and are in small denominations. The Chinese gentleman is offering a bribe to the captain to simply look the other way as some very illegal cargo is being loaded aboard. The captain isn't sure what may be contained inside the cargo container and doesn't want to know. He sees so many of those containers that one more doesn't matter to him.

The loadmaster for the Rosemarie has been rewarded for keeping his mouth shut and ignoring the plain cargo container as well. The container isn't very heavy suggesting electronics or something else that takes up space but isn't heavy.

The huge cranes make quick work of loading ships with thousands of cargo containers and the ship will sail for Los Angeles when the loading is complete. The crew are all busy preparing the ship for her journey and aren't aware of what's in any of the many containers their ship is loaded down with. The crew have been to many ports like this one in Hong Kong and have their jobs to finished before sailing. The cook goes down the check list shaking his head at the missing items. He knows his guys don't like rice and avoids that food at all cost. The first mate is reviewing numbers as quickly as he can but still certain containers get past him.

The load master is in on the deception like the captain and does a good job of hiding the fact that there's something not quite right about the container with no identifying numbers.

CHAPTER 2

The Big Lift Salvage and Lumber Company is recovering from deaths, damages, and losses. The two bad guys are existing on an island and cannot ever leave there. They are monitored electronically and someone checks on them monthly. The law knows nothing about the crimes that have been endured by Roses company. Rose, Jones, and Jack live in the big apartment in the Headquarters Building. The quarters are large with two levels and are quite nice. There are five bedrooms on the upper level and a huge Livingroom on the lower one. The apartment was designed to entertain and has spaces for hosting large gatherings. Jones and Rose haven't felt like entertaining anyone lately, they are just trying to calm down and handle all the big and small needs of Roses giant company. Rose has had a greenhouse built on the roof. She has a passion for growing roses, because her name is Rose. Jones hasn't been able to figure that one out, it probably doesn't really matter. If Rose is happy growing pretty flowers than Jones is ok with that. She grows some unusual roses and some that are more common. The greenhouse isn't large less than 18 feet by 80 feet, and is pleasant to visit.

Rose has asked Jones to take over more responsibilities in the company and he does. Jones hasn't a great deal of experience in big business, but he is a quick learner. Jones used to own and operate a dairy farm in Nebraska and farming is much different than shipping and logging.

Braidy is flying company aircraft, he loves flying and doesn't want to do anything else.

Nancy has married a man, Melvin who she met at her church. They live in an apartment building closer to Melvin's work at least for now. Nancy to her surprise, is expecting soon. She doesn't make rounds anymore since she is pregnant. She carries her baby well and stays in good shape. Melvin is in sales for a clothing distributer, and is a good provider. He wants Nancy to get out of the security business, it's much too dangerous he thinks. Nancy tells him,

"No, no way, I won't do that, keeping people safe is my life, I want to protect the people in this company. I have been working for Rose and her father before her for a long time, and am staying."

Melvin sighs and tells her ok, but he doesn't like it.

Carmen who was injured by some nasty creeps is becoming more responsible for logging and lumber sales. She doesn't allow her blindness to stop her from doing what she needs to do. She has become tough and still fare, she thinks over problems and renders her verdict. Her humor is evident in all that she does, and most people who don't get their way do get a laugh out of the encounter. She understands ideas of marketing and is able to work magic with buyers. She sells ship loads of hardwoods to everyone foreign and domestic alike. She isn't afraid to go out to logging camps and find out for herself what's going on. She seems so innocent, and guys like her but when she knows the facts, she rules with an iron hand.

Carmen requests Jones to fly her places, but goes with Braidy too. She has been to all the camps and knows the people there on a first name basis. Carmen has come a long way in her short life, she is now 23 years old. Rose marvels at the changes in her young friend, and is just plain proud.

Joni is still working down stairs at the front desk, she likes people and deals with trouble before it can make its way to Rose or Carmen. Joni still lives at Brady's house, and pays him rent for her room. Braidy has asked her out for a date and she has gone, but she says she still misses Don. Don was killed by Kenny; he is one of the prisoners on the deserted island with his partner in crime Marvin.

Jones visits them once in a while and reminds them of their crimes and of the danger they will face if they try to leave. The two are so cowed by Jones that they simply back away and say yes sir. Jones isn't vicious and doesn't like having to be the one who reminds them of the violence that he is capable of. He just wants them to stay on the island and remember the hundreds of people they are responsible for killing. Jones checks the electronics around the island to inform him as to their movement and leaves off another couple of months' worth of MRE's.

Kenny and Marvin haven't changed, they aren't reading any bibles for instance but they aren't thinking about any evil plots either. Of course, there are listening devices where they hang out, and Jones and Nancy analyze what they are saying once in a while. They don't care what Kenny and Marvin talk about as long as it's not anything dangerous.

CHAPTER 3

There is an island where Kenny and Marvin once made plans to take over and destroy Roses company. The little island has a village with around fifty people. The people are very pore and live off the land and from the sea. The dairy farm is also small with around 15 cows. The milk isn't sold to big dairy's, rather the locals sell to their own customers. The milk is clean and sweet, and the villagers take turns milking the cows and selling the milk products. On the other side of the island is a big house that apparently used to belong to gangsters or drug dealers. No one knows exactly who the house belongs to any longer. Jones has convinced Rose to simply buy the entire island which includes the house. The island didn't have a clear title but paying overpriced lawyers and bribing some folks did the trick. Roses company now owns the island and Jones visits the cattle herd occasionally. He milks the cows sometimes just for old times' sake. Rose is happy to give her man some piece of mind since his farm in Nebraska was destroyed by bad guys. Rose finds out that her father paid for burying everything on Jones's farm after everyone was killed. The big dozers moved in and dug huge holes and pushed trees, buildings, livestock, and everything else in to the holes and covered it all up. When the dozers were finished, there was only a flat piece of ground. The land was purchased by nearby farmers and is used to grow corn and beans. People who don't know wouldn't even know that there was a farm place there before the destruction.

Barbra is from Jamaica and has her own charter fishing business. She is tough and knows fishing, and does well during the fishing season. She is living in the big house and is able to check up on the village people. She has contacted Braidy and he is teaching her to fly.

She is especially interested in flying his float plane. She thinks a plane that can land on water and the land is wonderful. She knows about boats and other mechanical equipment and learns quickly. Braidy flies his float plane over to the island and she hops aboard for another flying lesson. Braidy is older than Barbra and isn't really expecting any kind of romance and is surprised. Barbra invites Braidy in for some of her good cooking. She settles him in a comfortable chair in the kitchen and talks to him while she prepares a fish dish.

Braidy usually cooks for himself and others he isn't use to having someone else make him dinner. He is impressed with her good nature and beautiful voice; she brings out the best of any music she sings. Braidy likes music but can't carry a tune even if he uses a dump truck, and so when Barbra sings, he listens. She is a delightful host and bubbles over with happiness. Braidy asks her.

"Are all people from Jamaica such wonderful singers and are they all as pretty as you?"

"Well I don't know about being pretty man, and as for the singing, yes sir, we all like to sing and be happy."

Braidy is an old dog and hasn't had much experience in the love department, but he does feel some strange sensations. Braidy is tall about 6 foot 6 and is a skinny guy. He has an eating disorder that requires him to feed often. He burns off calories rapidly and is always hungry for more. The people at Roses company know of his disorder and keep plenty of fuel for Braidy available. Jack especially enjoys Brady's disorder because what is good for Braidy is even better for Jack. Jack knows he can depend on good old Braidy for a quick snack.

Barbra smiles at her pilot friend and says,

"Hey man, you're gonna like this fish I'm cooking for you, and you can have your fill."

Braidy smiles big as the sky and licks his lips in anticipation. Barbra uses a special recipe from home, and Braidy notices that she is using a touch or more of Rum. She gets Rum shipped over from home, and has a good supply. She doesn't abuse it; she just enjoys some once in a while. Well more like once a day but who's counting.

Braidy is a good instructor and has taught many others to fly, he thinks that Barbra is ok too. She asks him if he would like to sit on the front porch for a bit, the fish has to cook for a while. She calls it cooking but she means the fish is soaking in some juice she has prepared. The fish will marinade for some. Braidy notices she has fresh bread she has baked and homemade butter. Barbra gets cream from the dairy and adds a touch of salt. She puts the cream in a mason jar and rocks it back and forth with her hands and in a short time the cream turns into real butter. Braidy discovers there's nothing like it, he is a connoisseur of fine food and appreciates Barbra's efforts.

CHAPTER 4

Barbra takes her boat to the mainland for fishermen who want to catch the big ones. She has a connection with a sporting goods store who list her services on their website and on flyers available to guys to take with them. She knows these guys pretty well by now, she can tell the ones who are serious about catching fish and those who want a good time. She charges lots of money for the little she does and always provides plenty of cold beer. She doesn't knock herself out fixing lunches, she provides the fixings and guys can make their own. She does offer her home baked cookies and coffee too. Some guys catch fish right away and it hardly seems worthwhile going all the way out just for one fish although it may be very large. She shows them the sights, like pods of dolphins and if she is lucky wales too. She has fixed the cabin cruiser that came with the island house and calls it her own. She has no idea who the boat actually belongs to and doesn't care now. She has refinished every wooden surface and painted the rest of the boat also. She learned how to work on the Diesel engine too and keeps all the machinery shipshape. She has a 20-foot runabout that she uses for personal use, and has maintained that too. She is mostly happy doing what she is doing, she loves the sea. Lately however, she decides she is tired of being lonely. She likes this big goofy man that is teaching her to fly. He is very shy and turns red often. She is gentle with Braidy not pushing. She really wants to know what he might look like undressed in her bed. She bets he has never had a woman before, what a terrible thing is that. She will fix that little problem or her name isn't Barbra. Braidy has no idea what's coming his way, he is naive that's for sure.

Braidy and Barbra enjoy the fine weather while it is available, often its rainy. The porch is as long as the house and deep. There is a swing they are both sitting on, and Barbra sets it rocking with a shove from her tow. She is sitting close to Braidy and their legs are touching. Braidy doesn't say anything but she can see he isn't use to that. She thinks Braidy likes her though, he is uncomfortable but doesn't move away.

Barbra tells him that the fish is ready to be cooked the rest of the way and is he hungry? Braidy is of course hungry and tells her that sounds good. She goes off to the kitchen singing one of her island songs. She waves him along and he gets up too and follows. Barbra is a good cook, Braidy knows cooking and appreciates her fish.

CHAPTER 5

Rose has been purchasing container ships painted in blue over darker blue and she thinks they look lovely. She is so tired of her father's favorite colors red and white. She doesn't go to all the christenings any more, she just cringes at the bills for their construction. She finds captains and crews from the experienced workers in her company. The ships carry cargos from all over the world and she doesn't always know what each ship carries. Rose trusts her captains and believes they will do the right things.

The Rose Marie is only a couple of years old and is traveling to places like China. There are so many manufacturers based in China that is difficult to know which company is what. She knows that there are thousands of containers and crews record numbers rather than the contents of containers. The Rose Marie is skippered by a captain Smith. That is apparently his real name, Captain David Smith. Rose has always wondered about someone named Smith, it seems funny to her. Captain Smith came to her company from another shipping company and is working out, with 15 years of experience. The Rose Marie is more than 1300 feet long and carries thousands of containers. The ship will arrive in California in three days and isn't unremarkable at all. The difference is this ship has one container that carries people inside. The people are mostly women and they are very young and starving. Rose has no idea of the trouble that is coming her way. Captain Smith does know, he was paid to simply look the other way.

When the Rose Marie ties up at Los Angeles. The Naturalization and Immigration police are waiting. Someone has informed the government folks. The container is identified and opened, there are dead girls, and those who are still alive are in bad shape. The container is filled with humanity and hasn't any room for anything else. The pore people are confused and don't know where they are. Rose is contacted as owner of the Rose Marie. Rose is thinking to herself, and says to Jones,

"Oh, dear God, how can this be?"

Jones wonders that too, how can a company minding its own business constantly get into so much trouble.

Jones tells Rose that he can handle this for her, if she is ok with that? Rose sighs and puts down her trowel, she has been amongst her roses in the greenhouse. She tells Jones she needs to go and find out what's going on for herself. Jones knows she will do the right thing whatever it turns out to be. Rose takes the elevator down to the office with Jones. Carmen is sitting at her desk; Ken's old desk has been removed. The desk was 20 feet across and not very useful. Carmen likes the spot under the windows where she and Jack use to sit when she was first blinded and has her new desk there. She is a slight woman weighing about one hundred pounds, she has gained a little weight. She dresses for success whirring dresses that are expensive but simple. She still has long hair that is curly and shiny. She stands only five feet tall but seems taller behind that desk. Actually, she has a platform she had built, to place her chair and desk on, and is taller. The platform is 3 inches taller than the floor and helps to make her taller than she is. Carmen stands up and comes over to Rose and Jones, Jack comes out of the kitchen too. Carmen doesn't use a cane in the office, she knows her way around without it. Carmen knows her people well and can tell that something is on their minds. Carmen comes to them and takes Jones's hand and asks,

"What she can do to help."

Rose takes Carmen's other hand and says," We got trouble again!"

Carmen looks like she just ate a lemon, and resigns herself to whatever is coming.

Rose says with a fearful shaky voice, "The Rose Marie has been stopped in Los Angeles because they found a container full of Chinese girls mostly starving."

"Oh, dear God, how can that be?"

Jones notices that Rose said the same thing after hearing the news. Carmen asks

"What do we do about that?"

"I am going down there to see for myself what can be done." Rose is determined.

"I can go too, and I'm not taking no for an answer." Carmen is just as determined.

Rose says to carmen, "Good, I was hoping you would want to help."

CHAPTER 6

By this time, Joe has taken over many duties and he and Joni will hold down the fort. Braidy is available too and will keep an eye on things. Jones can fly them down there in the King-Air . The company has two just alike now, painted in light blue over dark blue. The planes are kept out at the company hanger along with 6 other aircraft. Braidy keeps his float plane there that he teaches Barbra how to fly with. Jones and the two women will fly off with five lawyers along. Rose doesn't know what's coming and has learned to be prepared as much as possible. The lawyers are a mix of young and old and have studied differing fields of the law. They will meet with legal types and will head off potential law suits hopefully.

Jones and the others drive out to the hanger and the airplane is waiting for them fueled and ready for flight. The plane can carry twelve passengers and is comfortable. Each plane has a refreshment station and a restroom on board. Jones has flown for a couple of years now and is careful like Braidy teaches everyone he instructs. The mechanics are proud of the new airplanes and the helicopter too, they wash all the planes often and the King Air looks brand new. Jim who was the main mechanic has retired and fishes often. The new boss is Ben, an kids Just as much as Jim did. Ben stands by the cabin door like he is ready to take tickets from passengers. Jones says,

"Well Ben, what have you guys been wrecking this time, we only got eight victims for you all to experiment on you know."

"Well I don't know about us wrecking planes; you guys do a good job of that for us." Ben is holding out his hand ready for a ticket.

Braidy doesn't get along with Ben as well as Jones does, maybe there's something about an age difference. Jones trust these men, they do the job right, they can kid with ease. Jones walks all around the airplane touching where he can and looking under and over everything. At one point, he even goes over and kicks the tires. Ben asks,

"What the hell was that for, are you thinking of buying this beast?" Ben stands hands in pockets.

Jones knows that kicking tires tells him nothing except that the tires hold air. Jones pulls out his wallet and begins to count the bills, there aren't many. Ben tells Jones that he hasn't got enough, and he will have to borrow it again as per usual.

The guys open the door for everyone and the mouthpieces go on first. Jones wonders what's up with that, how come they go before the women? After everyone else is on board, Rose and Carmen climb the steps onto the plane. Carmen looks nice in a skirt with pleats and a frilly blouse, she where's her hair in a pony tail that falls down her back past her waste. She is proud of her hair and puts ivory combs in it to hold it in place. She is whirring a light perfume that is fresh and smells like flowers in springtime. Jones doesn't know what it is but likes it.

CHAPTER 7

Everyone gets settled and Jones and Rose are sitting on the flight deck, Rose doesn't fly but wants to talk with Jones privately. Carmen is in charge of the lawyers and will give them instructions. Giving lawyers instructions takes a will of steel and she is the best. Carmen can talk in a normal voice mostly; this new plane is very quiet compared to the old King Air. Jones goes down the check list with Roses help, and starts the engines. The plane is much easier to fly than the old one. Jones taxis over to the runway and stands on the brakes letting power build. Jones likes to hear the engines roaring before he uses them for the takeoff roll. After he lines them up, he asks,

"are we all ready?"

He hears no disagreements and slides the throttles ahead and they are off, racing down the runway and leaping into the sky.

Rose and Jones are using headsets for privacy and the others in the airplane cannot hear them. Jones levels out at 12000 feet and sets up the auto-pilot. Rose is talking about what they should do and Jones is only half listening. He is thinking about the pore women in the container. Some of them aren't even old enough to be called women, the youngest is only eight years old. Rose is crying now, even though she doesn't know any of those victims. She has deep feelings for her fellow man and at times like this it shows. Jones knows she will do everything and anything for those Chinese women.

Jones flies them into Los Angeles and touches down with a slight bump. They will have to find their own transportation to the ship. Jones and Rose with a little help from Carmen tie down the plane. There is a curtesy car waiting for all of them, and they are taken to ground transportation. Rose rents an eight passenger van and Jones drives them off to the pier. The ship is there plain as day, there is crime scene tape closing in the vessel. Rose says,

"This can't be good for company image, right?"

"Yup you're right Rose, we will have to fix everything when this gets finished or better during the fixing process." Jones looks all around the huge ship.

The ship is just sitting there, no one is allowed to unload or even leave the ship. The crew has to wait on board until the police are finished questioning them. Now is when the company lawyers need to do their thing and get these guys free. The crew have families who haven't seen them for a while, and Rose tells the mouth pieces to get at it and help her people get off the ship. They are good and worth their salt for a change, in less than an hour the crew have left the ship, although they each had to provide information. The cops want to know where all of them live and that someone will vouch for them. Rose gets right in their faces and threatens to sue. The lawyers cringe at that one, they don't want a law suit with the feds. Rose doesn't care, she cares for her workers and now it really shows. Jones wonders if he needs to put a leash on her and get her out of sight for a while. Actually, he is proud of her and tells her. Rose is a wreck and when no one is watching she leans against him. Jones knows his woman and reassures her with a quick hug.

So far, the charges are against the Captain, the first Mate and the ships load master. These men had to know what was in each container and on the one In questions the numbers don't line up with the manifest.

The Federal Agent is a man standing 6 feet tall and weighing 180 pounds. He looks to be in good shape, like he works out often. Jones thinks he is too big for his britches, and would like to take him down a peg. He has to gather himself in a bit, that sounds like junior high school talk. Boy, where did that come from, he wonders.

"oh well what the hell, it doesn't matter."

The guy says his name but he says it so fast that Jones didn't get it. Rose has his card so that's ok, he can ask her later.

The lawyers are talking to cops anyway relieving Rose and Jones of the nasty job. Carmen is demanding where the women have been taken to? No one wants to tell her anything, she is asking politely and Jones can see she is getting mad. She grabs one of the lawyers and tells him to find out. The man looks at her like she is nuts, and when he looks at Rose, he tells Carmen

"Yes Mam, right away."

He goes off after the vans that took the girls, or women away. He must have found out before where they had been taken. Carmen can be tough, even though she is a small woman she makes big noises.

The lawyer Carmen sent after the Chinese women comes back in a short while, and tells Carmen that the women have been taken to a nearby hospital. Carmen walks over to Rose and Jones and tells them what she has in mind. Rose agrees with carmen and says to Jones that she and Carmen will go to the hospital for a visit. The visit won't be pleasant that's for sure. Maybe a visit is the wrong term but it fits for now. Jones says for them to call on the satellite phone if they need him. Rose and Carmen set off; they have taken the rental van. Suddenly Jones realizes that he and the lawyers are stuck hear until they come back.

Jones starts for the bridge high above the main deck and is stopped by a cop.

"Sir you can't go there, please stay on the main deck." The policeman is only following orders.

Jones isn't as nice as he should be and says, to the flat foot, "I own this ship and will go where ever I please."

The cop looks to his commander and then decides to let it go, and tells Jones ok. Jones climbs the steps three flights up, and there is the fancy new bridge that is on all the new ships. This bridge doesn't even look like it belongs to a ship, it looks like something out of Star Trek. There are video screens all around and keyboards, and there is a slight hum. The ship is still alive apparently. Jones doesn't understand anything concerning modern ships, only that one can speak a command and the ship will respond, right? Jones decides to test it out and says,

"Ship turn down the air-conditioning," the ship repeats his command and he hears blowers coming on gently moving cool air.

Jones thinks, *I'll be dammed, maybe I should just tell the ship to get us out of here.*

Jones finds the Captains day cabin and is looking for papers or something concerning this latest cargo. Theirs none of course, the cops got everything and or maybe it's all in a computer.

Carmen and Rose drive to the nearby hospital and cannot visit the victims, everything is locked down near the women. Rose can't get near the people and is frustrated. Carmen listens as hard as she can and can't get anything either. Rose looks for someone she can talk to in charge, but there's no one. She has so much power and all that money but still can't get what she wants. The police are guarding the women and say to Rose and Carmen to back off. Rose knows that even their fancy lawyers can't help here. She says to Carmen they will just have to wait, and Carmen takes her hand and shares her disappointment.

The two women find a cafeteria and get coffee. Rose asks Carmen if she wants anything to eat, and Carmen says no thanks? Rose calls Jones on the phone and he tells her that nothing is going on the ship is still waiting at the dock. The customers will be getting anxious for their cargo. Rose says she knows, but there's nothing she can do about that.

The news people are hovering all around waiting for something more to print. Rose sees them in time and gets them out of the line of cameras. Rose hadn't thought that she would be in print concerning the disaster. She supposes that it had to happen sooner or later She just wants to live a nice quiet life, out of sight out of mind but no.

Rose and Carmen sneak out a back door of the hospital and drive back to the ship. By this time the lawyers are all finished doing what they can. The Captain has been taken away with the First Mate. She will have to provide them lawyers. Rose doesn't know if they are guilty or not, it looks that way now. The FEDS are wanting to talk to Rose and Jones and Carmen are there too. They say that Rose isn't in trouble, they believe she had no knowledge of what was in the container. They aren't even sure if the Captain should be blamed, the cargo container isn't on any manifest, it has no paper work. Rose wants to know how could it get on the ship? No one knows of course, and their will need to be lots of investigation. Somewhere in China the box was loaded onboard. The ship has thousands of containers so one more would hardly matter. Jones says,

"Ships don't load themselves and so someone loaded it on board."

By this time everyone is worn out and they decide to find a hotel. Jones thinks this hotel bill will be really big. Rose doesn't care, she wants to find out about the victims. The authorities won't say for some reason, and that's a mystery. There's something going on here and Jones thinks it might be time for some sneaky. Jones tells Rose that he and Carmen have something to do, and please don't worry. Carmen has no idea what Jones has in mind, but goes along. She and Jones have worked together for a long time now and she will follow his lead.

Jones tells Carmen that she will need to act like a lost blind woman. She tells him she is lost, there's no acting to it. Jones wants her to wander around the hospital using her cane but not knowing what she is doing or where she is. Carmen tells him that probably that's the dumbest plan he's ever had. Jones shrugs and tells her to think of something better. Carmen is loyal and says she will do it but she won't like it.

Jones drives them over to the hospital and Carmen gets out in front of the building. She doesn't look helpless enough Jones thinks, he whispers to her,

"Carmen, you look too good, try to look like you don't know what you're doing and are lost."

Carmen, says "I am lost and I don't know what I'm doing."

Carmen moves into the main door stumbling a little on the step. She thinks why would anyone put a step-in front of a hospital. Carmen, moves inside and is greeted by a volunteer worker. The nice old lady asks if she can help? Carmen doesn't know what to do, she thinks fast, and says she is looking for the Chinese women that were brought in earlier. The woman tells her right this way. Carmen is taken to another floor and their they are. A gathering of Chinese women talking and eating, the room is a large cafeteria. They are not all dead, some have died but not all. In fact, most are alive, and will recover. Carmen is relieved for Roses sake. The Chinese women are chattering and are hungry. Carmen knows nothing about Chinese but decides to move amongst them anyway. They ignore her like she was just another American hospital worker. She tries to hear something she can identify but nothing. Carmen wants to find someone to talk to about these women and circles around the room searching for a nurse. Finally, she finds the volunteer again and asks her?

"How many women are here, and how many didn't make it?"

The volunteer doesn't know. She tells Carmen it looks like there are over one hundred. Carmen calls Rose and tells her that she got right in no problem

Rose is saying she will be right over as soon as Jones can come and get her, Jones retrieves Rose and comes in the hospital with her. Rose doesn't understand why the secrecy, why make them wait for so long. Rose finds a charge nurse and starts asking questions. The nurse doesn't know anything either and sends them off to the hospital administration. Rose is nice now, knowing that she needs to find out information. The woman behind the big desk tells them that the INS will handle the problem and these people will be moved out soon. Rose gets the idea that this woman doesn't want these free loaders in her hospital.

Rose and Carmen are upset over the happenings at the hospital and don't know what to do. Jones tells them they need to wait for the government people to do their thing.

After a restless night, Jones flies them back to Seattle. The guys put away the plane and Rose drives them back to the office.

Rose instructs the lawyers to find out what will happen to the Chinese people next, she will help them if she can, even though what happened isn't her fault. The victims will need some kind of legal help, and she tells the lawyers to find out. They aren't happy, they just want to wait for the government to tell them what's next. Rose wants them to be proactive and make things easier for the people.

Jones is looking over the ship's cargo manifests, and isn't understanding what he is reading. There is documentation alright but not for the extra cargo box or for 11 other boxes. Jones asks Braidy to stop in when he gets in. Braidy and Jones will examine the paper work together and put everything in some sort of order. Jones can't say what it is, but there's definitely something weird.

Jones tells Rose of his finding or lack of findings and she looks too. She knows shipping more than Jones, and spots it right away. She says the cargo container that held the Chinese women is heavy. Even when empty its twelve hundred pounds heavier. Jones looks again, and asks her,

"How did you see that so fast?" Jones looks perplexed.

"Well I've done this for a while, and of course I'm smarter than you, ha ha." She tweaks his nose.

Jones saying ouch! nods, agreeing with her, he isn't a shipping magnet. Jones, is saying, if the container is heavier empty what can that mean? Rose tells him that she thinks the container has extra product inside, maybe in the floor or walls. Jones doesn't like that, and wonders how did the cops miss that one. Rose, tells him that it's easy to miss, the numbers aren't obvious. The empty weights and the full weights run together in most cases, no one really cares what the empty weight is just the full weight. The ship is supposed to be balanced out when it is being loaded. The cargo master wants to even out the weights to keep the ship on an even keel. Jones is asking her where is the shipping container now? Rose tells him that it's still on the ship chained down with the rest. They just opened the doors letting all the people out but leaving the box on deck.

Jones tells her that he needs to fly down there again and check out that container. Rose asks him if he will take Jack? Jones, tells her he will take Jack and Braidy both. And he will take his gun too. Rose doesn't like guns like her father and says that. Jones agrees with her, and tells her that he will leave the gun out of sight

CHAPTER 8

Barbra goes fishing nearly every day and tries to catch fish for herself and the village people. She isn't always successful and they have to buy canned food. The village people fish too, and do alright for themselves. Their biggest income however is the dairy. They take good care of their cows and keep everything clean. Still there are only 15 cows and sometimes some of the cows are out of production. The land won't support more than 15 cows so expanding the heard isn't likely. Barbra needs to be near people who like her and she helps when she can.

    She travels the 20 miles to pick up clients, and she shows them a good time. She is lively and kids with them, she knows most of the good fishing spots and usually can find them fish. She doesn't waist anything though, and keeps the very best places for herself and the villagers.

    Barbra enjoys living in her own house and invites people over for big dinners. The village people are happy go lucky folks and they dance in the big room. Barbra has enjoyed having Braidy over for dinner too and was disappointed when he didn't even try to kiss her. She decides that Mr. Braidy will take some time. She has her single engine rating for her pilot's license and will get her multi engine rating soon. Braidy is a good teacher and is exacting in his instruction.

    Barbra likes coffee in the morning and has purchased big bags of coffee from Guatemala. She grinds beans fresh and loves the flavor. She brings a big thermos of hot coffee on the boat with her and really likes traveling over the waves by herself in her own boat sipping good coffee.

Barbra reaches the dock and there are three big fat guys waiting for her. Boy why do these guys do that to themselves. The three men are grumpy and don't even return her good morning. She shrugs it off and welcomes them aboard anyway. The men are mean looking when she looks closer and aren't so fat. They are dressed too nice for fishing and Barbra gets suspicious. She keeps her father's big revolver handy and feels better. She asks them what would they like to fish for today? The guys are not talking, one pulls out a gun from a back pocket and before Barbra can get hers out gets the drop on her. The nastiest looking tells her they are here for their property. She knows exactly what they are talking about but plays dump.

"hey man I don't know what you talking about."

The bastard hits her crossed the face with his pistol and she falls to the deck. She wipes her mouth with her sleeve, and says.

"No man I don't know you, why you hit me like that?"

He tells her to drive the boat over to the island, and she thinks of asking what island but wisely decides not. She resigns herself to her fate and drives over to the island now their island. She wonders what will happen to the village people? Barbra brings the boat to the dock and the tough guy pushes her onto the dock. She hasn't given up yet, after all there are only three of them. She decides to use some of her island charm and out comes the Jamaican. They aren't impressed, and look at her like she is from somewhere else.

The three punks walk around the house looking for something. She has no idea what it might be, she knows every part of the property including the house. They move furniture and cut open chairs and couches too. The empty out cupboards and dump frozen food from the freezer. She doesn't even say a word, she can replace the food. She shrinks into a corner and tries to look smaller. Finally, they stop looking and turn to her. They will get nasty she knows, and prepares herself for a beating. The beating doesn't come, suddenly one guy says he remembers where it is. The others look at him with a question. He tells them that the box got hidden down the well. Barbra remembers that that crazy Marvin was dropping cats down that well, it won't smell to good that's for sure. They ignore her and go out the back door to the well. The well is 40 feet deep at least and doesn't have any water in it any more. They are gone and she slips out going toward the boat. One of the creeps sees her and tells her to stop. She looks back and sees the gun and stops. He tells her to come over towards him, the gun is steady and she moves over. She is forced to join the others around the well, she is surprised, the well doesn't smell bad. What happened to the dead cats? There are no corpses down in the well that she can see or smell. They want her to go down the well and find a box. Barbra asks how, and the nasty one hits her again. She isn't going to look very pretty for Braidy if this keeps up. She says she can get a rope from the boat and they can lower her down the well. The nasty guy sends his pal with her and she goes over to the boat and finds a long rope. The rope is new, she has never needed it. She thought it might come in useful for something she guesses this is it.

They tie the rope around her middle, and down she goes. Barbra isn't afraid of much, but she doesn't like going down the well, its dirty and not very wide. The well was dug by hand, and must have been dug by a shrimp. She gets down to the bottom and wonders how to find the box. She pokes around while she stands not knowing what else to do. She asks them for some sort of tool, to poke around with. One of the nasty's drops a hammer. Barbra, saw it coming and managed to catch it before it smashed her on the head. She used the claw part of the hammer to pry rocks loose, the rocks came right out, like they hadn't been in place very long. She finds that more of the rocks come loose and theirs a big hole behind the missing rocks. There is the box, right in front of her. She wants to take a look inside of it, and wonders if she could get away with it. The nasty guy says to her,

"Did she find the box?"

Barbra decides to just tell him she has, and she wants to know what to do next. They tell her to tie the box to the rope and they will pull it out. She ties the rope to a ring in the top of the box and up it goes. The bad boys pull up the box and exclaim when it is opened. They are ecstatic and forget all about Barbra. She calls out to them and one simply drops the rope down to her, the problem is he untied it at the top. Barbra is stranded in the bottom of a well, she can't get out. The bad guys move off with their box and soon she hears the

Diesel engine start on her boat. Barbra thinks well at least I'm on my own land. Barbra tries to climb the walls using her body to press against either side of the well. The walls are crumbly and she falls back down the foot she has gained. She is trying to think but panic is setting in and she begins to despair. If only one of her village people came by, she wonders if they ever come over here anymore?

CHAPTER 9

Jones and Braidy fly down the coast with Jack, they fly low because of Jack's ears. Jack howls in pain when they fly above 5000 feet. He does like the new King air however, it's much quieter than the old one. Jack has a new cushion to lay on during these really dull flights. Rose had a new one made, it is the new colors, blue over darker blue. Jack resigns to his fate and settles down with a sigh. Jones and Braidy are armed, they both have practiced behind the hanger, banging away at cans and bottles. They are getting better like two old west gunfighters. They don't use holsters on their hips, but do use holsters behind their backs. They don't like guns at all, but know that it can be a dangerous world.

After landing at Los Angeles international airport and tying down the plane they rent a car. The ship is still docked where it was, nothing has happened with the cargo. The insurance is the problem now, although no one knows why. Jones is asking Braidy,

"What is the matter with the insurance company?"

Braidy replies, "It's probably because of potential law suits."

Jones sighs and says "Everyone is suing everyone else for everything."

Braidy wonders at that statement, and tells Jones he's probably right.

The ship is quiet, the power has been turned off, and there is only the waves lapping at the ship. They meet the security people that Nancy has hired to guard the property and go aboard. The cargo box in question is there alright and the doors are still open. Jones shudders to think of more than 100 people living in there for 8 days. The cargo box smells like dirty humanity and Jones doesn't wonder, what a way to see the world. Braidy starts knocking on the various sides of the box, he has a ballpeen hammer from the plane. Everything sounds solid. Braidy asks Jones what are they looking for? Jones doesn't know, he tells Braidy that he will know it when he finds it. Braidy keeps on tapping. When he taps on the floor, there is a different sound in the middle. Jones comes over and looks at the floor. Jones tells him to tap all around to try and determine the shape of the hollow spot. They decide there is definitely something alright but it doesn't sound hollow, and it's about 3 feet by 5 feet. Jones tells Braidy they will need some pry bars or crow bars. Braidy looks around helplessly theirs nothing. Jones says this is a ship there must be a bunch of tools somewhere. Braidy turns and there are three nasty looking guys pointing nastier guns at them.

Jones looking more pissed than frightened, exclaims "Oh shit!"

Braidy doesn't move, he knows these guys got the drop on them and don't look like they would hesitate at all. The guns aren't even simple hand guns, they are machine pistols. The stubby guns have clips with lots of extra bullets just in case the first 25 don't do the job. Jones looks for the security people, they are all gone!

Jones is concerned, where is Jack? He was sniffing around the ship but isn't anywhere. Jones was focused like Braidy on the container, and doesn't know where Jack has got to. The three bad boys don't talk, they just motion them to come out of the container. Jones and Braidy come right on out, there's no point in guarding something they don't know anything about.

After Jones and Braidy come out of the box, the three bad guys move them towards a van parked on the shore. Braidy groans and remarks that it's a red van with white trim, you know like the old colors. Jones shakes his head, what a thing to think about now. The nasty boys take their guns, that was easy than tie them with those ever-ready zip ties. Jones holds his arms stiff trying to keep the ties looser, and one guy notices and hits him on the back of his head with his weapon. Jones falls down, and doesn't pass out. He wonders why he doesn't get mad, like before, could it be he has lost his special powers? Then he remembers that Braidy is near, he believes that he doesn't get mad seeing red when friends can get hurt.

Jones can't out run a bullet, and even if he could, Braidy certainly can't either.

They are driven off, and they weren't blind folded.

CHAPTER 10

Rose calls Jones and gets no answer, and the same with Brady's phone. Rose tells Carmen that she has a bad feeling and wonders what they should do? Carmen has come to depend on the two men, so when there are times like this, she can't think for herself. Rose calls Nancy, and fills her in on the two missing guys. Nancy had her baby and stays at home. She still works for Rose and plans on coming back to work. Nancy's husband doesn't like her working in security and tells her he can find something in his company for her. Nancy likes action and the adventure of security and tells him no thanks. Nancy tells Rose she will get a baby sitter and come over. Carmen is listening and tells Rose that she can watch the baby. Rose mentions that to Nancy and she says,

"if it's no bother, it would get me there faster, just let me pack up what you will need, thanks Carmen."

Carmen is excited thinking about babysitting Nancy's baby, she has to ask Rose, what the baby's name is and what kind is it. Rose tells Carmen that she thinks it's a Ford. Carmen exclaims,

"oh, you know what I mean??"

Rose takes Carmen's hand for an instant and says she's kidding of course.

Since Nancy has gotten married, she had to find another kind of car. No more sport car, instead she and Melvin have a SUV with enough room for the baby, the dogs, and the people too. Nancy gets her baby all strapped in and the diaper bag, food, bottles, and her gun. Nancy kept her gun even though Melvin doesn't like it. Nancy is loyal to her friends at Roses company and the need to help is strong. Nancy arrives at the headquarters building and the guard on duty recognizes her, he also sees her baby and asks about the kid. Nancy tells him she's a girl and will most likely grow up as beautiful as her mother. The guard claps his hands and says,

"That's a good one, you're probably right."

Nancy uses her key card to enter the private elevator and she and her little girl are whisked to the top floor. Nancy is organized and does it in one trip. She bustles in and Joe whistles at the baby. He says what a beautiful baby. Nancy says does he mean me or my daughter? Joe isn't dump and comes up with both naturally. Carmen and Rose come to the office door and help Nancy with her baby and her equipment. Carmen is careful and holds the baby just right, she cradles the girl close to her chest and Nancy is ok with Carmen's care. Rose is admiring too, she can't remember the babies name and doesn't want to ask, there was a baby shower and they sent gifts. Finally, Nancy mentions that the baby is also name Nancy. Rose says of course I knew that! Carmen shakes her head a tiny bit, reminding Rose that she had forgotten. Nancy wants to know all the information about Jones and Braidy, there's not much. Nancy decides she will fly down to Los Angeles to find out more. She wants to know if Jeff can go along, she may need some help. Jeff has been with Roses company the longest of any of the other security employees. Rose trust Jeff, and tells Nancy that's a good idea, she will feel better about Nancy if Jeff goes too. Rose calls Jeff on the building wide paging system and the sound of her voice wakes the little Nancy. Carmen has been holding her and looks alarmed at the baby's loud cry. She keeps it all together though and soon has little Nancy quiet.

Nancy tells them that they call the baby Nance and maybe that will lessen the confusion.

Nancy contacts Mac at the company hanger and asks him to get the other King Air ready. Nancy and Jeff are discussing the trip and she tells him to bring a vest, two guns, and some of those zip ties. They will use the new radios; they can use them for two- ways between themselves. Jeff is ready and brings extra bullets for their automatics. Rose doesn't like the look of guns or extra ammo but keeps quiet. She knows that they may be dealing with bad guys again, Rose knows that this crap will never end. There's something about managing a multibillion-dollar company that invites trouble. She will deal with these creeps like all the rest. Rose has gotten tougher and has had to make decisions that may seem cruel but are still so very necessary. She misses Jones and is worried about Braidy too.

Nancy and Jeff go down and check out a company car and Jeff drives them out to the airstrip. Nancy checks out the airplane and they both climb aboard. Nancy has flown many planes including the one they are using and is comfortable with each one. She waves at the mechanics and lines up on the strip, she looks at Jeff and off the go.

After landing in Los Angeles, they make their way to ground transportation and rent a midsized car. Jeff has his phone and is directing them to the ship. The GPS isn't necessary, the harbor is easy to find, but it's what they always do. When they arrive at the ship, Nancy and Jeff look around and call out for Braidy and Jones. They hear a dog whimpering, and discover Jack, he is behind a stack of containers. Jack has been struck on the head and is groggy. Nancy gets down on the deck and holds his big head on her lap. She is looking him over, and finds a bullet wound in his hip too. Jack looks bad, and she needs to get help for him soon.

Jeff has had training in medicine and takes over. Jack is conscious and licks Nancy's hand; she is reassured by that little gesture. Jeff pulls out a small first aid kit they all carry now and applies anti biotics on Jacks wounds. There is lots of blood but the bleeding has mostly stopped. The head wound is an open cut that will need to be stitched. Jeff talks to Jack all the while; he is gentle telling Jack what he is doing. Jeff doesn't know if animals can understand him or not, but it seems to help. It's probably just the sound of his voice rather than what he is saying. Jack is a good patient and holds still. Nancy is ever vigilant even though they are working on Jack her eyes are always moving and she is listening. Nancy was taken once by surprise and she has vowed she will never be taken again.

CHAPTER 11

- Barbra has been shouting as loud as she can but no one hears. She is about to give up and just die when an idea occurs. She looks at the hole where the box was and lifts her foot high and pushes her tow into the cavity. She leans on the side of the well and steps up. She rises up 3 feet, she is elated by this and looks around for the hammer, she dropped. She looks and looks and can't find it, and is annoyed by something in her shorts pocket that is in her way. She reaches down to remove it and then discovers the hammer in her pocket. She shakes her head, and thinks, *she is going crazy.* Barbra reaches to the wall with the hammer and taps on a rock that is part of the wells lining. She knocks down another rock that falls below her. One by one she pulls out rocks and makes a series of holes she can use to step in and pull herself up and finally out. She has never felt so much relief in all her life as when she rolled out of that well. She just lay there for a moment breathing fresh air and looking at the sky. Barbra gathers herself and remembers the danger she is in. She holds the hammer like a weapon now not a tool any longer. She will smash those assholes into paste when she catches up with them. Barbra moves around the back of the house and looks toward the dock. The big boat is gone, and the smaller one has been set adrift. She can see it about a half mile out to sea. She thinks some and remembers that nice life- raft that Rose gave her. She has replaced the paddles and even has a small electric motor on board. She has to inflate the raft; she has stored inside the boathouse. She needs to use a hand pump to blow up the raft and after almost two hours the boat is good enough. She mounts the motor and creeps over the water toward the runabout. The boat has drifted further out to sea, but still insight. Barbra doesn't know what made her recover this raft but now she is really glad she did. She gets to her boat, and finds the spare key she keeps under the seat in a metal holder. The boat starts right up and she toes the raft back to the dock. She hasn't got her father's gun anymore and decides to borrow one from the village people. They haven't much, single shot rifles only. She can drive her runabout faster than she can walk, and she zips around to the back side of the island. The people are around doing what they do and aren't surprised to see Barbra. She talks to the other women first; she believes that she needs to follow protocol. Talking directly to the village elders is a two-stage process. She could talk to them directly and could get away with it, but why cause trouble. Everything in the village belongs to the village and so she must ask everyone. The village people are glad she is alright, they tell her that they will fill that well in with rocks and dirt. They tell her that they climb down the well and removed the dead cats. Barbra is happy about that; she blames herself for what happen to island cats. They tell her no, not you; it was that bad man named Marvin. She tells them that that bad man Marvin is gone for good, he will never bother them or the cats again. They ask why does she need their gun? Barbra tells them that she needs the gun to defend herself, while she finds those bad guys that took her big boat. They tell her that they have only 3 bullets for their gun. She says she will buy more when she comes back and then they will have plenty. They all agree that's a good thing and give what they have. Barbra waves and goes to her runabout. She has a good idea where to go to find her other boat. She guns the throttle and heads for the mainland. She notices that it's getting dark, and is ok with that, she has come over many times in the early morning darkness. She uses her GPS and the compass to navigate her way with. She gets to the mainland in an half of an hour and finds her cabin cruiser tied up at the public dock. She thinks, that was easy, and now what about the bad guys. She looks all around and there is no one. She ties her runabout to the back of the cabin cruiser and climbs aboard. The boat is like she last saw it, and she even finds her father's revolver, she may not need the village rifle after all.

 Barbra unties the cabin cruiser and takes both boats back home. She drives both boats into the boathouse, ties them up and locks the outer doors. She walks a crossed the lawn to her house, what a mess, cushions have been ripped open drawers emptied, books destroyed everything torn apart. She doesn't want to think about it, and instead opens a new bottle of that good Jamaican Rum. She doesn't even bother with a glass, drinking it right out of the bottle. She feels the warm roll down her throat into her belly. She sighs in contentment and has another just because.

Barbra decides to wait until another time to clean up the mess. She will sleep on her boat for this night and gathers up what she needs.

CHAPTER 12

Braidy and Jones are driven to an old garage used for repairing cars. They don't know what's coming next but know it can't be good. Jones is worried for his friend Braidy and tells him they'll get out of this somehow. Braidy is a good sport, and says,

"Yeah man, we will!"

The bad guys haven't said a word, just pointing and gesturing. Jones is looking for an opportunity to jump them but none comes. Braidy is scared, he isn't use to being kidnapped and needing to defend himself. Jones has had combat training but hasn't had to use it for years. They are shoved into a room that is dark and are locked in. Braidy is asking why didn't they just kill us? Jones, tells him that he is glad they haven't. We still got a chance to find out about Jack and maybe hurt these bad boys. Braidy agrees, that's a wonderful idea, and how do we do that he mumbles.

Braidy is asking, "Isn't this what happened to Nancy?"

Jones tells him it is,

"So do we start singing Amazing Grace?"

Nancy sang loud and strong when she was captured that allowed Jack and the guys to find her. Jones wonders what happened to Jack, is he alright, did they kill him. He is sad about that thought, and thinks about something else. Jones thinks of Rose and their life together, he has never known such happiness since he has been with his Rose. She will find a way to get us out of this mess. Jones asks Braidy,

"Say old man, how did those creeps find us there so easily?"

"I don't know, I'm just the airplane driver after all."

Jones doesn't remind him that he flies too, and says,

"Yup you are!"

Nancy and Jeff and now Jack are slowly moving over to the rental and will take Jack to a vet. Jack is able to move on his own, slowly though. Jack is a tough mutt and is recovering. He is becoming stiff, mostly from the bullet wound. The bullet when clear through his left hip and will need stitching. The cut on his head will need at least 10 stitches to close. Jack is looking an sniffing however and is mostly himself. He is a dog on a mission and needs to find Jones and Braidy. Nancy and Jeff watch Jack walking around the ship and on the shore before getting into the car. They have no idea what happened here but know that Jack can do extraordinary things. Jeff says,

"Say Nancy didn't Jack find you when you were kidnapped?"

Nancy says feeling small, "Yes, he did, I was singing really loud and he heard me, although from what Jones tells me, Jack was on my trail before that."

Jeff, tells her that he hopes that good old Jack can do that again.

CHAPTER 13

Barbra decides to call Braidy and when she gets no answer from his satellite phone, she calls the company hanger. The guys at the hanger tell her that he's not there. She wants to know when he will come back? They tell her they don't know. Barbra decides to call that woman Rose, she still has a card she gave her. She calls Roses private phone, and Rose is surprised when her giant handbag begins to ring and buzz. She forgot she put it in there. She looks at the caller ID and doesn't recognized the number. She answers it anyway, and hears a voice she has heard before. Barbra's Jamaican accented lilt comes bubbling over the phone.

Barbra sounding hesitant,
"Excuse me mam, I be looking for that Braidy fellow."
Rose says,
"Is this Barbra, from the island?"
Barbra says "Yes, it is and ask her how she is?"
Rose, is polite and tells her ok, and, how is she? When the niceties are finished and out of the way Rose asks,
"Barbra, what can I do for you?"
"Oh not much, I am looking for that Braidy man."
Rose tells her she doesn't know right now; they have been looking for him. Barbra decides to tell this Rose about what happened to her. Rose gasps, after hearing about Barbra trapped in a well, she tells Barbra to come over if she likes, to the company headquarters building. Barbra says she doesn't have a car, and can't get a crossed to that building. Rose tells her that someone will meet her at the dock and will bring her over, ok.

When Barbra gets to the office, she sees Carmen holding Nancy's baby and just has to admire. She tells them theirs a baby with a good color. At first, they are shocked and then after looking at Barbra who is medium brown in color agree with her. Rose and Carmen are listening to Barbra's tale of trouble and shake their heads, and wonder what's it all about now.

Nancy and Jeff are helping Jack, they have taken him to a vet. The Doctor exclaims,

"Wow, what a big boy you are, and you have gotten yourself into trouble I see."

Jack licks his hand with his giant tongue, and the vet smiles at the people,

"His tongue works!"

Nancy says that Jack is part of their security team and was injured in the line of duty. The doctor looks at Jacks hip than at his head. The hip wound will be stiff for a few days but will heal. As for the head wound, I will need to sew it up. He asks Nancy if Jack has any allergies? Nancy says she doesn't think so, he's actually not her dog. The Doctor tells them ok, and prepares a syringe for Jack. The pain killer is a local and will numb his head. Jack doesn't even move when the doctor slides the needle in. The doctor tells them that this is a remarkable dog. He is probably the biggest dog he has ever treated. Most of his patience are small dogs suitable for lap sitting. Jack gets the nasty gash on his head sewn up and the bullet hole on his hip closed as well. Jack knows he is finished and offers the vet his paw. The vet exclaims,

"What a nice dog you are, I've never met a dog quite like you!"

The3 return to the ship, and Jack wants to explore some more. He moves to the container that held the Chinese women and sniffs his way to the edge of the dock. The ship is large and just walking around on it takes some time. Jack stops where the van was parked, looks south and barks at Nancy. She gets it, and has learned not to ask Jack stupid questions. Jack waits until they bring the rental car and then move stiffly down the street. Jeff asks Nancy if she thinks that dog knows what he is doing. Nancy reminds him of her rescue when Jack tracked her to that warehouse where she was held captive.

Jack goes for a short block looks all around and then sits. Jack has lost the sent, he doesn't know which way to go.

Jones and Braidy are still locked in the small room, the room must have been used to store tires, the smell is still strong, they are talking about their situation. Jones sighs and wonders,

"I don't know why they are keeping us alive, and who are these guys?"

"I don't know man, and I don't know why they should care what we do with that container." Braidy wipes his face with his big paw.

"There must be something hidden inside the floor of the container that they want, and they don't want us to know what it is."

"Well, you're right, and by the way, how do we get out of here," Braidy is kidding sort of, "how do you get mad and bust heads and doors?"

"I don't know, it just happens, maybe I'm not mad enough, or we aren't in enough danger."

The door is flung open, and there is two of the bad guys with their nasty guns, what in the hell are those things? One motions with his hand and tells them to come with them. When Jones gets to the door, they force him to turn around and his arms are pulled behind his back, and he is tied. The same treatment happened to Braidy, and then hoods are slipped over their heads. The two men are pushed out the door, and across the garage floor to another room. This room is set up as an office. The man behind the desk is dressed in a pin stripe suit and wares a bow tie. He has polished finger nails and has his hair fixed just so.

Some say that he may have his hair colored too. He is polite with a pleasant voice requesting them to please sit down. He offers them refreshments and Braidy is tempted but declines. The man says he has their ID's on his desk, and knows who is who. He looks at Jones and says,

"so, Mr. Jones, I understand you used to be a farmer?"

Jones doesn't even bother wondering how he knows and tells him yes. He continues and you Mr. Braidy have flown for Big Lift Shipping for 35 years? He continues, saying to them that they have interfered with his business, and he is not sure what to do with them.

He doesn't say anything about the Chinese women, rather is referring to the hidden space in the container. You gentlemen are sticking your noses where they don't belong. Jones isn't afraid of this little creep, and thinks really bad thoughts at him. The thought goes unnoticed however, the man continues.

"We had a nice little thing going with the women and the other until you ruined it."

Jones is getting mad and wants to ring the fancy bastard skinny neck. Fortunately, Braidy speaks calmly and the man responds.

"We had a good thing with Ken, and could transport almost anything on the old bulk carriers. When the container ships came along it seemed like it might be even easier."

Jones says, "Well we don't know exactly what you're talking about, we had no idea what was inside that container, not even the women. And as for the other, we don't even know what it is, and for that matter who you are?"

"You will never know who I am, the question is, what we do with you two? If we let you go, you will contact the police."

Jones with a smirk, says, "That they cannot contact the police for anything, you see we have our secrets."

The man is interested, and asks,

"Say what, what do you mean?"

Jones tells him that good old Ken, was a crook in more ways than one, and cleaning up his messes taken some doing, for example flying way out over the ocean and dumping unwanted led weights with bodies attached. The guy grins at that one, and says,

"Really, and how many of these trips were there?"

Jones says, "I could tell you but then I'd have to kill you!"

The fancy man continues, "So if you got secrets and we got secrets maybe we can work something out. I know your boss owns lots of these container ships now, and we can offer some kind of deal."

Jones starts to get mad, not red mad but Jones mad, he won't allow this fancy pants to cause any trouble for Rose. Jones says,

"No way, we are a legitimate company and want nothing to do with scum like you."

The two bad boys behind them lift their machine pistols ready to blast them into tomorrow. Fancy pants waves them down, and motions them to return Jones and Braidy to the locked room.

CHAPTER 14

Nancy and Jeff with Jack are driving around the dock area and Jack is sniffing the air, although he isn't having any luck. Nancy and Jeff know there's not much chance of finding any kind of sent in the city. Nancy says they should go back to the ship and look for some more clues. Jeff agrees, and she drives them to the ship. Jack is out the door and moving over to the container that the Chinese women were in and is pawing at the middle of the floor of the container. Jeff looks at Jack, and Nancy has her gun out and up, she doesn't like the bad feeling she has. She has vowed to never be taken by surprise again. She is looking all around and Jack is standing next to her. Jeff looks at the floor and tells her that he thinks there's an outline of a compartment built into the bottom of the container. Nancy doesn't turn to look at him, she is vigilant. Jeff goes over to the rental car and searches in the trunk for a jack handle. There is one but it's not much. He tries anyway and finds that the cover comes up easily. He removes a piece of thick ply wood revealing an opening below. There is a metal box lying flat between the supports of the container. The box has no markings and is plane metal. When Jeff tries to lift it out, he cannot. Whatever this box is, it is very heavy. Jeff lays the ply wood cover back and comes over to Nancy and Jack. Jeff has his gun out too and while looking all around with Nancy explains what he has found. Nancy says,

"We're going to get more help than us, there's something bigger than just trafficking illegal Chinese women."

Braidy and Jones are sitting on the floor with their backs against the wall. They are staying mostly calm and are discussing what Mr. fancy pants said. Jones,

"The man must want something from us or Roses company, I mean besides transportation of illegal aliens. Braidy wonders how come those women get into a box like that in the first place? Jones tells him that they are wanting to get out of China or are holding a family member for ransom. He doesn't know, there can be many reasons, those people are living desperate lives back home. Sometimes reaching for a dream calls for extraordinary measures. Braidy tells Jones that he is using bigger words since he has been living with Rose. Jones knows his friend is kidding and goes along.

"So, big boy, do you miss me?"

Braidy sniffs a bit and says, "Yes, I do, although Joni is nice to have around."

Jones is asking if there's anything going on between Joni and Braidy? Braidy turning his usual red, admits,

"Well I would like there to be, but so far she doesn't want much to do with me."

Jones scrunching his but around to get comfortable says, "I understand she is still grieving after Don, maybe in a while it will work out."

Braidy sighs and hopes so too.

CHAPTER 15

At the headquarters building Barbra, Rose, Carmen, and Nance are enjoying visiting in spite of the circumstances. Barbra is charming with her Island humor and she and Carmen are getting along delightfully well. They have discovered they both have wicked senses of humor. Carmen keeps up with Barbra and Rose is left in the dust. The two women can talk about anything it seems Carmen doesn't want to allow Barbra to dwell on her injury resulting in blindness, and skillfully avoids the subject. Rose is the observer and watches the two exchange jokes and even recipes. Rose hears her phone ring and answers in the nick of time before it goes to voice mail. It is Nancy calling them, she tells Rose what they have found on the ship, and will need more help, she tells Rose she doesn't like any of this. She also tells her that Jack got injured and is ok. Rose feels like one of her people got injured when she hears about Jack. Nancy tells Rose what she knows and Rose says she will get on it right away.

 Barbra is asking if that's where Mr. Braidy is? Rose tells her yes, he is, but we aren't certain where yet. Barbra doesn't want to admit how much she cares for Mr. Braidy, but to herself she calls him her man. Nancy tells Rose that both King Airs are parked nearby and Jeff doesn't fly. Rose hasn't thought of that, she expects that the boys would fly her planes home themselves. She feels panic when she thinks of losing either one of them. Rose tells Nancy to hire some detectives to watch both planes. She knows it will be expensive but worth it. Jeff and Jack are walking around now Jack has his nose down and his tail up. He is sniffing around the container and moving out in a bigger circle. He stops sniffs looks back at Jeff and moves on. Jeff is watching this unusual dog with interest. Jeff has a dog at home but nothing like this mutt. Nancy is ever watchful; she won't be taken by surprise. She has been scrolling through information on her smart phone. These little phones are like miniature computers having gigabits of information available at her fingertips. She finds security companies that offer guards for hire. She hires 12 people and provides information for payment. The company will provide two for the planes and the other 10 will come to the ship. She insists that the guards be well armed. The dispatcher doesn't like the sound of that. She says that will cost extra. Nancy gets demanding, and tells the woman that she is the customer and demands that the guards be armed.

CHAPTER 16

Mr. Fancy Pants actually has a name, and his hirelings call him Mr. Nice. Mr. Nice is not the biggest cog in the gear but he's pretty far up there. He knows what surely must be in the box in the container but doesn't want anyone else to know. The thugs are just hired bad boys and enjoy burgers fries, and killing innocent people. They aren't very smart but follow orders witches what Mr. Nice likes.

Mr. Nice needs to retrieve the box when no one else is around, even the thugs can't know what's happening. He doesn't like unfinished business but can't kill Jones and Braidy quite yet. He may need to negotiate with that Rose sometime soon. Rose and Carmen are still talking with Barbra and of course Nance. They are getting worried about the two guys and Rose begins to pace around the office. Barbra notices and tells her that she will help. Rose looks at her and wonders how? Barbra, tells Rose that she can fly, thanks to Mr. Braidy and will just fly down there to that Los Angeles place and get him back. Rose is surprised at that, she had no idea, she asks,

"How long have you been able to fly?"

Barbra tells her that she has been taking flying lessons from Mr. Braidy for more than a year now, and she flies good too. Rose tells her that she doesn't doubt it at all. Rose calls the hanger and asks if there is a plane that they can use or are they all gone? Ben is gone but Mac is there, and answers,

"Yes, there is the Cessna and of course Brady's float plane."

Rose thinks that would be something to rescue Braidy with his own plane and his own newly trained pilot too.

Rose doesn't explain anything to Barbra, she needs to think it over. What good would it do to be down there too, what could she do that's not already being done by Nancy and Jeff, and who can forget Jack

Carmen guesses what Rose has in mind, and asks, Rose,

"What should they do about Nance here?"

Rose wants to leave Carmen home but knows she wouldn't like that at all. Carmen needs to be included in anything that involves Jones or Braidy and especially Jack. Rose calls Joe and asks him if he feels comfortable watching the store for a while? Joe is ready willing and able, and says he can. Rose calls Joni at the front desk and asks her to come up for a minute please? Joni is up in a moment, the elevator they use for employees only is fast and there's never any wait time. They each have a key card they use on the elevator and doors too. Joni has her own and is there ready and able. Rose asks her with some hesitation,

"If she likes kids?" Joni gulps and notices Nance for the first time.

Joni is probably too old to have her own even if she had someone to help her make one. She has nothing against kids though and admits that she hasn't been around many children. Carmen is an old hand at kids now and tells Joni that there's nothing to it. Joni sits down on a chair and Carmen lays Nance in her lap. Joni blinks back a tear and swallows a lump in her throat, there are feelings coming out she didn't know she had. Joni likes the feel of this little bundle and soon gets the hang of it. Carmen explains about changing diapers and Joni isn't worried about that. Carmen tells her that soon she will get a chance to change Nance and just then a nasty little stinky comes wafting out from the precious little bundle. Joni does get it and isn't bothered at all. Rose smiling at Barbra saying to her,

"Ok Barbra, you're on, if you think you can, let's go please."

Barbra jumps up and says,

"Hay hey ok let's go!"

Rose Carmen and Barbra drive out to the company hanger. Mac is there and has the Cessna one-eighty out and ready. Barbra has flown this plane with Braidy and knows all about it. She is inviting, and opens the doors for everyone, and Carmen gets in first. There are four seats in this small aircraft and the cabin seems very small.

Barbra is going through the check list just like Braidy has shown her. She gets everyone in and seat belts fastened and starts the engine. The plane like all the others has been well maintained and is filled with fuel. Barbra has never flown to Los Angeles but she is confident and lines up on the runway. She asks if everyone is ready like Braidy does and everyone is. Barbra advances the throttle slow and easy like Braidy and they are off racing down the runway and into the cloudy sky.

    Rose has been around company planes all of her life and is impressed with Barbra's flying, she is smooth and rotates off the runway with style. Rose remarks that Barbra is a good pilot, and she can tell that Braidy taught her. Barbra smiles at Rose, and tells her that Mr. Braidy is a good man, and Rose can tell that Barbra means more than a teacher. She thinks, oh ho, *'a romance in the works.'* Carmen is using her smart phone researching something, that girl can find on that little phone more information than most people can on a grownup computer

CHAPTER 17

Jack is moving around the ship; he is stiff and needs to keep on moving to prevent the injury from getting stiffer. Nancy has the hired guards spread out around the dock area and the ship too. Jeff is watching Jack and is noticing some little things that the dog finds. Jeff doesn't know what they will do with information that Jack discovers, he just observes. Jack isn't finding anything significant; he is going through the motions. Jack looks at the box and then at the bridge and upper decks. He can't say what he is thinking, that is if Jack does think. Whatever goes through his mind has captured his interest? Jeff hasn't worked with Jack before and so doesn't know what he can do.

Barbra lands smoothly and Rose helps her get instruction to a place to tie down the plane. Barbra catches on right away and follows a follow-me truck. The truck leads them to an area for private planes to park. They get a ride from an airport van to the ground transportation center. Rose rents a small sedan and drives them to the dock. She has been to the facility before and doesn't need direction from Carmen. Carmen has her GPS app up and says she can offer Rose directions. Rose says,

"thank you honey, its ok I've been here before."

Carmen closes the app and goes back to searching for something else. She uses a blue-tooth headset and is quiet.

They arrive at the ship and see the guards all around and are challenged.

"may I see some I.D. please?"

Rose doesn't mind a bit; she offers her driver's license and says she is the boss. The Woman looks up in surprise and says excuse me mam. Nancy waves them over onto the ship and meets them

Nancy is surprised to see Barbra there, and looks at Rose. Rose tells her that Barbra has been learning to fly from Braidy and has flown them down here. Nancy is wondering about her baby, and Rose tells her that Joni is babysitting. Nancy knows Joni and relaxes and says that's alright. Rose says that Joni is staying in the office and has plenty of help if she needs it.

Barbra is looking all around this huge ship, and has eyes as big as saucers. She wants to know how many them boxes are there? Rose tells her thousands and each box holds tons. Barbra asks about the open container and is told that there were Chinese women being held in there for 8 days.

Barbra is shocked and asks,

"Why?"

"You see Barbra someone made those women get in the box in China and they were brought here." Rose is reluctant in what she says.

"Do you mean they had no food or water?"

"They each had some of their own we think, and some didn't make it, I mean some died." Rose blinks back tears in her pretty sad eyes.

Barbra,

"What kind of man do that kind of thing to people like that?"

Rose explains about trafficking in young women and that she had no idea it was happening on her ships. Barbra looks very sad and the look is so unusual that she appears to be a different person. Rose takes her hand and says that they will fix everything for all these Chinese people.

Barbra is asking about Braidy, and Nancy tells her that they think he and Jones have been taken away by bad guys. Barbra looks all around and asks,

"How can that be" My Braidy has gotta be somewhere."

Rose looks at Jack and Jeff exploring the ship and asks,

"You guys find out anything new?"

"No mam, I'm not sure what we are doing, I'm just watching the dog. Jeff looks uncertain."

Barbra looks up and all around and asks,

"Do you see those little camera things up there pointing down at us?"

Rose looks up to and says she does. She says to Barbra, "Excuse me dear, I don't know what you mean?"

"Well maybe those little cameras were watching when they took my Braidy away don't you know?"

Rose remembers that the cameras on all of her ships run on an independent circuit. The cameras don't need ship power to function, they have their own power source. She also remembers that each camera has its own memory that is separate. They can look in the camera's and maybe see what happened here, the police wouldn't know anything about the extra precautions. Rose looks at Barbra with admiration and tells her that she may be right.

Rose instructs Jeff how to retrieve the memory chips from the camera's and he brings 4 of them down to Rose. Rose uses a special player with a small screen and runs the video. When they get to current time, they see Jones and Braidy taken away by gun point. Barbra gasps when she sees her man being carried away in that red van. Rose sees that too but also notices there is a shot of the license plate on the back of the van. Nancy sees too and says she can use her magnifying glass to make the image larger. Rose looks at her and says,

"Why Nancy is that a real honest to goodness spy glass?"

"yup it sure is, I got from one of my special spy places and use it all the time."

The van does have a license and after lots of squinting they can read it. The license is a California plate and Carmen asks for it. Rose doesn't wonder about Girl Wonder and her magic phone any longer. Carmen has gotten an app that allows her to look up license plates too. Carmen tells them that the van belongs to a repair garage with an address. Rose can't believe it could be that simple and asks Nancy if it could be? Nancy doesn't know, she would have to contact someone in motor vehicles in the state offices. Carmen brings up her GPS app and has directions to the garage. Jeff and Nancy want to go right away and find the garage and maybe rescue Jones and Braidy. Nancy has needed to pay back the favor for her own rescue by the two men. Jack comes over and sits close, he is really stiff and sore. The hip wound swells more than his head wound and he has trouble moving. Barbra comes over to Carmen and looks at the screen and asks,

"Hay girl, how you do that on the little thing in your hand?"

"Its magic don't you know."

Carmen holds her phone for Barbra to see, and Barbra holds Carmen's hand to keep it steady and in focus. The phones app is clear and has the route marked out for people to see and use. The app can provide verbal direction while someone is driving.

Nancy is no coward and will do her job; she isn't as foolish as she used to be, thinking of her baby. Nancy needs to talk to the hired guards. She gathers some of them around them and tells them the situation. These guys are young and eager to help. She knows that none of them have ever been in a real gun fight or even been shot at before. She hasn't had a lot of experience but she was shot twice now and knows that hunting bad guys is dangerous.

Rose wants to keep their past out of this, but she thinks they might need some help from the local cops. Nancy says to Rose that the first thing to do is go there and find out if the boys are there. Rose is asking how? Nancy tells her that Jack can go along

Nancy wants Jeff, Jack and Her to go there by themselves and check it out. Barbra doesn't like that at all and says so. Nancy asks Barbra if she has had any kind of training with guns? Barbra shakes her head no, and looks denied. Nancy knows that this is no time for being soft about anything. She and Jeff are experience with guns and other tactics. Nancy has worked with Jeff on other jobs and knows he is reliable and will follow orders. Barbra is a different story; she may be to impulsive. Rose doesn't want them to separate, and suggests that they all go, and some wait several blocks away. After all they brought the radios and can stay in touch. Nancy agrees and they will take both rental cars. Jack needs a little help getting into the van and Jeff gives him a boost. Jack lays down on the floor and rests his head on his paws. Carmen climbs in with Jack and she rest his head on her lap. She strokes his head being careful to avoid his injury. Jack doesn't feel well, he aches all over and his nose is hot. Carmen talks to him in their special way and Jack sighs.

Rose drives the van with Jeff navigating using Carmen's phone. Nancy and Barbra take the sedan and go first. Jeff is using the radio giving directions to Nancy, the radio lays beside her and the sound is loud enough to be heard. Barbra is excited over finding her man, but also actually doing something. She tells herself to be careful, after all those bad guys got the drop on her on her boat. For sure she doesn't want to end up in another well, that was terrifying and she shivers at the thought of it.

The little convoy travels through the city and soon are in amongst industrial businesses. The stores are auto parts and plumbing, lumber companies and other commercial type properties. Jeff tells them that they are five blocks from the garage now and probably will want to stop. They find a parking lot with space behind a hardware store. Nancy decides to drive the van to the garage, it has a bigger engine and is higher up in the air. Nancy looks at Jack and decides to let him rest, he is sleeping with his head-on Carmen's lap. Carmen loves this dog and wants to protect him. Nancy asks Jeff what he thinks and he suggests that they walk over first.

Nancy asks Jeff if he is ok with this investigation? Jeff is ready and it shows on his face, he checks both guns and pats the extra ammunition clips in the combat harness he wears. Nancy has provided them with every device and piece of equipment she can find and they are ready. They are wearing the new style vests that are better and can stop bigger bullets, at least they are supposed to. Nancy was wearing a vest when she was shot once and the vest did stop the bullet but the bruise took two weeks to heal.

Nancy and Jeff walk down the sidewalk like they lived around there and no one noticed. Jeff spotted the garage first and sees a red van parked in front, the van looks like the one in the video from the ship. Jeff whispers to Nancy,

"Nancy, that looks like the right van, the one we saw in the video."

"Yes, it is I think, what do you want to do?"

"Well you're the boss, right!"

"Oh yeah, I forgot, well let's just watch for a moment. That's what Jones showed me out in the woods."

"That sounds good to me, and we can change our minds."

Nancy knows he is kidding but pokes his chest with her stiffened finger. Jeff tells her,

"Ouch!"

They watch and wait, nothing is happening, no one comes out, no one goes in. The place looks deserted, the lights are on inside however, its daylight

CHAPTER 18

Back at headquarters building, Joni and Nance are getting along famously. She is enjoying the interaction with Nancy's baby; the little girl is a happy baby not making much trouble. Joni understands this little one better than she thought she would. Nance is still very small and cannot move much on her own. She can lift her head some but can't be put on the floor. Joni feels strong feelings that she didn't know she had. She supposes that every woman has those maternal feelings and it takes a baby to bring them out. Joe is at the main desk on the ground level and calls the office. Joni answers the phone one handed and says hello to him. Joe tells her that Nancy's husband Melvin is on the phone. She asks him what does he want? Joe tells her that Melvin is wanting to know where his wife is? Joni, utters a colorful word She tells the baby,

"Oops, sorry about that."

The baby doesn't mind and lays on her lap comfortably. Joe continues,

"Melvin says he will come over and get his baby, and if that Nancy is gone chasing bad guys after he told her not to, she's in big trouble."

Joni sighs and says she will get Nance ready to go with Melvin. Joe is not liking the sound of this at all. He tells Joni that he will bring Melvin up to the office himself. Joni tells him thanks and continues to gather up Nance's equipment. She thinks it certainly takes a lot of stuff for one small child. Joni gets everything ready before Melvin gets there and is just sitting with Nance enjoying the feel of the baby.

Joe lets her know that he and Melvin are coming up on the elevator and their they are. Melvin is in a temper and sounds aggressive and mean. The baby picks up on that right away and starts to cry. Joni has held her for hours with hardly a whimper and this Melvin comes in and the baby howls. Melvin is a tall black man standing over 6 foot 4 and is built like a brick house of comfort for outside use. He sees Joni's white cane and really loses it,

"You mean to tell me that my baby has been watched all this time by a blind woman?"

Joe isn't a small guy either and comes between Joni and Melvin. He is younger and solid. Joe knows Joni well and won't put up with any of Melvin's bad mouth at her. Joe says,

"Just cool it, you can't abuse Joni here, she has done a good job taking care of your baby."

Melvin doesn't back down, and raises his fists. Joe doesn't like the look of that, he backs up a step, and says to Melvin,

"I know the martial arts and don't want to have to hurt you."

Melvin sees Joe in an impressive stance and thinks twice about it. He says he's sorry, and it will never happen again."

Joni is feeling hurt and holds the baby closer comforting her. The baby quiets some with that and Melvin notices the change. Joe straightens up and says,

"Hay man I think you owe Joni here an apology."

Melvin says he is sorry again, and admits that Joni is doing a good job after all," he asks, "where is Nancy?"

Joe thinks at last they are getting to the real problem. Joe doesn't hesitate, and tells Melvin that Nancy has flown to Los Angeles with Rose to take care of some company business. Melvin gets heated up all over again and kicks a chair out of his way. Joe thinks, *'it's better he kicks a chair rather than him or heaven forbid Joni.'* Melvin asks,

"When will she be back, and how can I get a hold of her?"

Joe says that he can't talk with her right now, they are busy. Melvin is trying not to be mad but is shaking with anger He doesn't like anything about this dammed company and wants Nancy to quit before she gets hurt again. Joni holding Melvin's baby close says,

"I know about people getting hurt, my Don was killed by some bad guys because of what happened with the owner's father."

Melvin looks at Joni curiously and wants to ask what she means but is too embarrassed because of what he said earlier. Melvin isn't a bad fellow; he is just worried about Nancy.

CHAPTER 19

Nancy and Jeff decide to move over to the garage and try and listen and maybe see something through the grimy windows. Nancy motions for them to spread apart and Jeff goes left and she right. They simply walk normally over towards the old building just like they had business there. No one moves and nothing happens, and Nancy points to the door. Jeff nods and steps over. Jeff tries the handle and the door swings open. He looks in and then back at Nancy shaking his head slightly. He is saying there's nothing there. Jeff takes one step inside and is hit by dozens of bullets from both machine pistols. Jeff is dead instantly; the gun fire has turned his face into something unrecognizable. Nancy ducks around the edge of the building out of sight. She is shocked and shivers, she is terrified, thinking that maybe Melvin is right. She can't think about that now, she swallows hard with fear. She has two guns, both automatics but nothing compared to machine pistols. She will need to come up with a different plan.

Jones and Braidy hear the gunfire and jump to their feet. Jones tries to sense what has happened but nothing comes to him. Braidy asks,

"what was that?"

Jones tells him that was those machine pistols on full auto, shooting at something, whatever they shot at is probably very dead. Braidy shutters and sits back down on the floor. Braidy is tall and he is a long way from the floor. Jones goes over to the door and even though he has tried before he tries again. The knob doesn't turn and the door is shut tight.

Mr. Nice comes out of the makeshift office asking,

"What in the hell do you assholes think you are doing?"

Mr. Nice isn't so nice now; he shows his vicious side and belts the closest gunner. The bad guy is knocked cold falling on his back on the floor. Mr. Nice use to be in boxing and still has a very effective uppercut. Just for an instant the other bad guy raises his gun pointing at Mr. Nice. Just for that instant Mr. Nice thinks he is a Dead man. He gets himself together and barks orders.

"You stupid bastards, get this trash out of here, and I mean now!"

Mr. Nice is afraid of dead people and can't stand having anyone just lying about. The bad guy gets the third man and together they drag Jeff out and then behind the building. There is a dumpster with a cutaway side and they get Jeff's body up and in. Nancy peaks around the corner of the building and sees Jeff being tossed away like so much trash. For a moment, she wants to lift her gun and kill both but restrains. She doesn't know where Jones and Braidy are yet, she needs to get them free first then kill the bad guys.

In the van, Jack lifts his head off Carmen's lap and looks towards the garage. Jack has heard the gunfire, and he knows that someone is in trouble. Jack slides out the door that is still open and begins to move down the street. Carmen calls him back, but Jack just starts to run. The rest seems to have renewed Jack and he moves easier. Rose is calling Jack too, neither woman can stop Jack, he has something on his mind and won't be detoured.

Nancy is hiding close to the corner watching and waiting, she needs more information. Nancy nearly jumps out of her skin when something wet and big pokes the back of her knee. She turns ready to shoot and sees Jack sitting back on his big but grinning at her. She is so relieved that she smiles at the big dope. She remembers the danger she is in and points in a around the corner motion, She wants them to go behind the building. They will be out of sight from the front, and she looks Jack over. His nose isn't hot anymore and there aren't any leaks to worry about. Nancy is actually glad to see Jack and says so. Jack does his usual thing and licks her very sweaty hand. Nancy wonders if Jack can tell where Jones and Braidy are, and simply asks.

"Hay Jack, do you know where the guys are?"

To her surprise, Jack walks to the building and stops at a spot half way along the back wall. Jack looks at the spot than at Nancy and then back at the spot again. Nancy after looking all around moves over to the spot taps the wall with her gun but. There is a returning tap from someone's shoe maybe. The tap is loud enough for her to know that it is one of her guys. Nancy moves back away from the building with Jack and looks at the problem from a different point of view. She thinks to herself than asks,

"Jack how we gonna get them out of there?"

It was a good thing they moved out of sight, just then two bad guys come around the corner of the building to light up smokes. Mr. Nice doesn't like smoking and makes his thugs go outside for their bad habits. They lean against the building where Jack indicated the guys are. The cigarettes they light are king-sized and look twice as long as the regular kind. Nancy doesn't know much about cigarettes though and settles back with Jack who is panting slightly in her ear. Even though Jack is injured and can't use a gun she feels better with him with her. She wonders how her baby and Joni are getting along. She hasn't any worries about Joni's baby care, she just thinks about it. The bad boys with the smoking habit crush out their smokes and move back inside the garage. Jack looks at Nancy and then at the wall, he is asking what should they do. He isn't really asking of course its Nancy's interpretation only. Nancy thinks to herself, *'what should they do, and should she get more help?'* She looks at the dumpster where Jeff is, also theirs a wrecker, several cars, some with missing body parts and an old-school bus. She wonders for a bit if the wrecker could bash in the wall, and if she can start it without a key no doubt. She decides to wait and see what develops next. The bad guys were only two, what happened to the third one? She wonders how many others are inside the building?

Jones and Braidy heard the tapping on the outside wall. Jones thinks that it is Nancy out there. Braidy,

"what is Nancy doing here, I thought she would be home with her new baby?"

"Maybe she got a baby sitter, I don't know, but that was for sure Nancy's knock, we have our own that no one else uses."

Braidy looks at the wall some more, and asks,

"How do you think this wall is built, are their wooden studs like a stick-built house or something else like steel studs?"

"I can see wood studs with stucco on the outside and this metal on the inside. We can break through the stucco I think, but the metal inside will be the problem." Jones looks at the screws holding the metal to the studs and looks around for some sort of tools. If they could get a few out, they could pull the metal off the wall with both men trying. Braidy looks too, they can't find anything like a screw driver there isn't any tools or loose objects.

At the parking lot behind the hardware store Rose and Barbra are going crazy with worry. They thought they heard gunfire and are really scared. Barbra says to Rose,

"I can't wait no more mam, I gotta know what happened to my man, I'm gonna go over there."

Rose can see the Barbra has a huge gun she pulls out of a big bag she has been carrying. Barbra has her father's revolver and is loaded for bear. Rose doesn't like guns and says,

"Barbra, do you know how to use that big gun?"

"Oh yes mam I do, I got this bad boy from my father, and he showed me how to shoot, I shoot good too."

Rose also wants to know, and agrees to sneak over for a quick look. She tells Barbra that they will only look, no funny business. Barbra says nothing, non-committal and simply walks off in the direction everyone else has gone.

CHAPTER 20

Melvin has left with Nance and her equipment. Joni and Joe can tell that he isn't used to dealing with the baby. He isn't really certain how to hold her but finally does almost get it right. Melvin says he will ask his sister to help him with the kid. Joni is still in the office and Joe has gone back down to the main desk. Joni answers the phone when Joe calls,

"hey Joni, there is someone calling about cargo from the Rose Marie, they want or rather are demanding delivery or release of the containers and right now. Joni, hasn't dealt with problems like this on an upper level position but certainly knows how to deal with mad clients. She tells Joe that she will handle the call. Joni answers the phone like she owns the joint. She even sits at Carmen's desk and lowers her voice. She says,

"This is the big lift shipping and lumber company; how may I help you?"

The caller isn't polite, he wants to know where in the hell his containers are? Joni, wants to know his name and what company he represents? The guy is really starting to boil, and swears at her. Joni plays it cool,

"Sir, if you're going to use foul language with me, you'll have to make an appointment with our lawyers." Joni has used this line before and the guy becomes submissive and is polite. Joni thinks, *'that's better.'* She doesn't know anything about the containers in question and so will fake it from now on. She says to the man she will need the information facts to her, when she has that she can respond to his questions. The man agrees and asks for the facts number. Joni does know one and repeats it for him.

The day at the company is finally coming to its end, and Joe calls her from below. He tells her that there is a fax and what should he do with it. She tells him to bring it up please and wants him to read it to her. Joe locks the doors and closes the business for the day. Employees have been leaving sneaking out early like they always do, Rose knows and once in a while scolds them. She keeps track of who works hard and who slacks off.

Joe comes up and notices that there is still some coffee left and helps himself. Joni and Carmen have been talking some and Carmen told her that there are 11 containers unaccounted for in the paper work from the Rose Marie. When Joe arrives, she asks him to look for the missing files and he finds it right away. Jones had been looking also, she wants to know if the fax information concerns one of the containers without paper work. Joe finds it; the facts indicates that all 11 containers have the same numbers. Joni still smiling remembering the baby asks,

"What does that mean, how can 11 containers have the same numbers?"

Joe study's the fax and the information of the unknown containers and says,

"I don't know what's going on yet, but these 11 containers that seem to be missing have the same numbers and contain the exact same cargo. The cargos are the same and the numbers are too, but nothing really exists. There are no containers and the numbers don't apply to any container."

Joni, "What numbers do the container that had the Chinese women in have?"

Joe, "According to what Rose found out, that container has no numbers, the numbers have been painted over or have been removed."

CHAPTER 21

Barbra and Rose are hiding behind a building a crossed the street from the garage, Rose is terrified and Barbra is excited. Rose sees Nancy and Jack crouching behind a parked car. Nancy looks over toward Rose after Jack pokes her with his nose. Nancy and Rose see each other, and Nancy waves her back. Rose ducks back behind another building and then Nancy sees Barbra too. Nancy says to herself,
"oh hell, what are they doing here?"
The door to the room they're in is flung open and there are the three bad guys with their guns. The one who was knocked cold by Mr. Nice has a swollen jaw and doesn't look too good. Jones looks into their eyes and sees right away they have come to kill them. Before he realizes it, Jones has smashed them into paste, and Braidy didn't even see it. Jones doesn't even feel any regret this time, the guns made all the difference. Anyone who needs guns like those doesn't deserve a second chance or even a first. Braidy isn't bothered this time either, he is sick of bad guys beating the shit out of this company for nothing. Jones and Braidy step over the mess and go looking for Mr. Nice. They hear a car roaring off into the distance, Mr. Nice doesn't want to hang around, he has heard of Jones's violence. Mr. Nice actually wanted to force Jones to do a little cleanup work for him. Jones and Braidy walk outside and Rose and Barbra see them and come running over a crossed the street. Rose is in Jones's arms trying to climb inside him so happy that he is alright. Jones just picks her up and holds her against his chest saying its ok over and over.
Barbra grabs a hold of Braidy and pulls his big head down to her for a long deep kiss. Mr. Braidy doesn't even try to defend himself, and

finds he doesn't mind. Jack comes around the building, sitting still has made him stiff again and he needs a little time. When they get back to the parking lot and the rental car, Carmen is wild with anxiety and needs to know if everyone is ok? Nancy is crying, she has to tell them Jeff was killed by the bad guys. Rose is very upset and gets mad all over again. Jones reassures her that he got the bad guys that killed Jeff. He doesn't know which one killed Jeff, it doesn't matter, their all dead.

Rose is wondering what they should do with the dead guys when there is a fireball that use to be the garage. Mr. Nice has taken care of the problem for them. Jones suspects that Mr. Nice was hoping that he and Braidy would be in the garage along with the three musketeers. Jones thinks,

"Boy, this Mr. Nice isn't so nice, he plays for keeps."

Braidy rubs his big paws together and sighs

"now that's what I like, problems that take care of themselves. And by the way we need to leave right now, before the fire department arrives to put out a fire that is already destroyed the building."

Jones helps his dog into the van with Carmen, she holds his head in her lap like before. Jack is a tough dog, and will recover in time. Nancy and Barbra with Braidy drive the sedan. The day is long gone now and they are all exhausted. Rose doesn't want to push it and suggests they stay overnight in a hotel. Barbra says she's good, and can fly ok. Nancy wants to be with her baby right away, and Jones says ok too. Rose nods giving in, she wants to go home too. They arrive at the airport and return the rental cars. Braidy is surprised theirs no damage and they actually get their deposit back. No bullet holes, no dents, no broken glass, we're getting better at getting attacked. Jones,

"what did you say, I'm not sure I got that one?"

Braidy tells him never mind. Braidy asks,

"how did you get here?"

"she answers him sweet as can be, Mr. Braidy sir, I flew down here just like you taught me, and I flew good."

Rose concurs, and says,

"she did, and if you don't stop getting into trouble Mr. Braidy sir, she may replace you as bigshot pilot around here."

CHAPTER 22

The three planes take off from Los Angeles International Airport and Rose is admiring her little flock of blue over blue aircraft. The company name is on all of them and she thinks people will certainly know they were here after all that. She and Jones are flying with Jack and Carmen in one King Air, and Braidy and Barbra are in the second, and Nancy is flying the Cessna. The King Airs are much faster than the Cessna and so the entire flight is slower than flying without the smaller airplane. Rose has called the office and Joni is still there on duty. She has raided Brady's stash of goodies in the small kitchen and brewed herself a big pot of tasty coffee. She sits at Carmen's desk and feels like a queen, she likes the raised platform, only forgetting about it once. She makes herself a giant Dagwood style sandwich and says,

"here's to you Mr. Braidy, I'm having one of yours."

Ben has been waiting for them at the hanger, he worries about his airplanes and when there are three of them still out, he is terrified. Ben learned from Jim mostly and has some of the same values as Jim. Ben has talked to Jones on the radio and knows where they are. Recently they have installed lights along the runway. The lights aren't the same as at major airports, there aren't any lights on the runway itself. However, along the edges and at the end are enough lights to outline the runway. The runway is asphalt and stays firm even in rainy conditions. Ben hears them before he sees them, and listens to the engines with a professional ear. The King Airs just roar, but the Cessna sounds like a piston engine, mostly because that's what it is. Jones and Braidy want Nancy to land first, and fly in a circle until she touches down. She rolls on over to the hanger and steps down from the plane. As soon as she steps down from the plane someone comes out of the dark. Nancy is tired and has let her guard down, she isn't expecting anything here. Some man runs up to her and slugs her hard enough to knock her down. The man is Melvin, he is really mad and takes it out on his pore wife. He has left the baby with is sister and wants to punish Nancy for disobeying him. Nancy is just lying there she has been knocked out cold. Ben has seen what happened and runs over to confront Melvin. Ben is a smaller man and is slightly older but turning wrenches everyday has given him plenty of strength. Ben doesn't like big men beating up on small women and takes a swing at Melvin. Melvin goes down like a tall pine in the forest after the chainsaw does its work. He falls over on his back and lay still. Jones, thinks, well that's justice I think, she gets knocked down and then he gets knocked down.

Rose is shocked and covers her mouth, she doesn't like violence of any kind and seeing Nancy knocked down by her husband has taken its toll. Ben is rubbing his knuckles he will have a soar hand; he bends down and touches Nancy's face. She has a bloody lip and will have difficulty talking for a while. She comes around though and he helps her to her feet. She looks at her husband, he has gotten up on his own and starts to swing at Nancy again. Before Ben can stop her, she shoots Melvin right between his eyes. The trouble is, good old bastard Melvin doesn't know what hit him. The King Airs have both landed and everyone gets out and comes over to Nancy and Ben. Carmen is helping Jack down from the plane; he is having trouble walking. She takes her time with him and finally they are down. Rose looks at Nancy, and Nancy notices the gun in her hand and lowers it. Melvin is quite dead, the bullet hole doesn't even blead much. Braidy and Barbra are standing with their arms wrapped around each other, they are in shock too. Jones gathers in Rose and just holds her. Ben and Nancy are looking at each other and Nancy begins to cry out. She is more concerned about her baby than herself. She will need a good lawyer that's for sure. Jones thinks over the problem and will discuss some ideas with the others. Jones,

"now look you guys, Nancy was attacked by that peace of shit Melvin there, we saw it from the air but Ben was closer. Ben says,

"I didn't know he was hiding behind the hanger, I believed I was the only one here."

Jones says to Ben,

"you couldn't know he was there; he was behind the building and you were watching us, you're not to blame."

For now, let's get this guy out of sight, and think about what to do. Nancy is shaking with regret; she wants to know what will happen with her baby? Rose goes to her and tells her that they will take care of her baby don't worry. Carmen crying too comes over with Jack in toe, and tells Nancy what a beautiful baby little Nance is, she says she has never felt so good taking care of anyone like Nancy's little girl. Nancy feels a little better after that, but still is terrified. Jones comes over to Nancy and hugs her too, he tells her,

"hey Nancy, remember when I carried you in the woods after you got shot? I will carry you now too, believe me we will help you through this."

Nancy is overwhelmed and starts in again with tears, she just thanks Jones.

The guys bundle Melvin in a tarp and store him for the night in a locked truck behind the hanger. The truck is there since it broke down and is needing to be junked or rebuilt. The truck isn't needed for much and can just stay where it is for now. Everyone needs to rest especially Jack; he isn't feeling so good. Jones and Braidy lift Jack up and into the company van. There is enough room behind the seats for him to lay down. Carmen gets in with him and holds his head in her lap. Jack sighs and closes his big brown eyes. He may be hamming it up just a little, but still he was injured. Carmen talks to him in that special way she has and Jack drifts off to sleep.

Jones and Rose are getting ready for bed finally and are talking over the day. Rose is amazed that so little time has passed. She doesn't ask Jones about the head smashing in California, she is only glad that he can save himself and others. She has grown her blond hair longer, it's shoulder length now and is golden in color. Rose has a perfect figure, and even though Jones has been through the works he still admires his woman. She sees him looking and shyly smiles at him. She says,

"Mr. Jones, what are you looking at, and what do you want of little old me?"

Jones doesn't want anything, he is counting his lucky stars, what a perfect woman his Rose is, he tells her he is admiring fine art that's all. Rose slips on a pink nightgown and dives under the covers. Jones doesn't where anything to bed, he believes in personal freedoms at least under the covers. Jones will have trouble sleeping this night, the three bad guys will haunt his dreams. He doesn't know what makes the head smashing happen and cannot predict when. Today he thinks was ok, the bad guys were going to kill Braidy and him. He could see it in their eyes. They were about 1 second from buying the farm. He thinks, now where did that come from, maybe it means buying a cemetery plot or something. Rose is sleeping soundly; she is tight against him trying to get inside him he thinks. She is so small but so large. She weighs 120 pounds and stands 5 foot 3 and has the most perfect figure Jones has ever seen. He has known women before in his life but none like Rose. Jones wonders what they can do for Nancy. He knows the killing that he is responsible for will get no recognition, they were no bodies, but Melvin had a job and relatives too. Jones thinks about arranging some sort of accident, the problem is the bullet hole between his eyes. Why did Nancy have to be such a good shot, anywhere else could be explain easier. Finally, after 3 in the morning Jones drifted off.

Carmen and Jack are resting in Carmen's apartment, she finally convinced Jack to boost himself onto her bed. She hugs Jack close to her, and listens to his breathing all the night. Jack doesn't have any trouble getting to sleep, the Doctor has provided some sleep aids for dogs, and Carmen helps Jack get one down. She believes this dog is magic and can think thoughts that ordinary dogs can't. Jack snores like a dog and passes some of the gas he is so famous for, Carmen just smiles, and holds her nose. Boy oh boy, at least your tummy works, and everything after too.

Joe and Nancy go over to her sister's house to get little Nance. Joe likes Nancy and admires her; he helps to make up a story about Melvin. The sister isn't that close to Melvin and says,

"Oh hell Whatever."

Joe helps Nancy carry out the equipment and tells her that Rose told him she and Nance could stay in the headquarters building. There are several apartments available for guests and Nancy and her baby settle into one for the night.

CHAPTER 23

In the morning, they all meet in Roses office to talk about what to do with Melvin. Barbra is there too, she is involved. She and Braidy are sitting close, staying in touch, literally. Rose wonders where Barbra stayed last night but is too polite to ask. Barbra is not one to miss a golden opportunity and invites herself to Brady's house. Braidy had a pleasant surprise and looks contented. Barbra saw what happened too and offers a solution. Rose looks at this woman again with a new view. Rose encourages her to continue. Barbra tells them,

You know I take gentlemen fishing and sometimes go out pretty far, and well if something happens way out there who's around to know. I can provide the paper work, what do you call it, oh yes, the contract. Mr. Melvin just hired me to take him fishin and while he was out there fishin he falls over board and too bad, a shark gets him before I could kill the shark. I just got my father's old revolver you know."

Jones and Rose look at Nancy, Nancy looks at Jack, Jack licks Carmen's hand, Ben sips more coffee. Well it could work, Braidy likes it better than flying out with the new helicopter for a big swim 3000 feet below. We all never can talk of this again; we need to agree to that. Ben says he can tell the men to come in late if that will help. Braidy says,

"all we need to do is load that dead guy into the float plane, and Barbra and I can fly out to her island. We can slide the bundle that is actually Melvin into her boat and go for a little fishing trip."

Barbra is ok with that,

"and you Mr. Braidy will come with me on my boat, you know to help, I'm just a little oh island girl, I can't possibly move someone as big as a dead guy. Jones doubts that, he believes that Barbra can move mountains if she wants them moved. Braidy says ok and they all gulp down the last of the coffee and head for the hanger. Rose groans to herself,

"man, oh man, if all of the company secrets ever come out, I will be in prison for about 10,000 years."

CHAPTER 24

Mr. Nice looks back at the fireball that was the garage. The dead bodies won't be a problem after that big fire. He needs to get over to that ship and collect the box. The box is heavy but not 1200 pounds. The container has led weights inside the walls and roof. He wanted to give the illusion that the container was heavier empty than what the actual weight. His box weighs about 50 pounds. Mr. Nice is good at fooling people; he talked that captain into looking the other way when the extra container was loaded aboard that ship of Roses. The ship still has security around it that the black woman hired. They aren't very intelligent and he thinks he can convince them that he works for the INS. He has the phony documents and looks the part, well at least he thinks he does. He will tell them that he needs another look at the container that held those China dolls and the box will be in his hands. Mr. Nice has played, the police, FBI, a doctor, ship's captain, port inspector, and oh well, anything and everything. He does have a college education and most people don't know about it. He has a Master's Degree in Sociology He has never used his education for anything but crime but what does it matter, at least he makes a living, right.

Braidy and Barbra drive out to the hanger and Melvin's remains are still there. The night was cool and he hasn't changed much. It is still very early in the morning and no one is around. Braidy doesn't like this body removal business. Barbra is a good helper and lifts the other end of Melvin. They have wrapped the body in a plastic tarp and tied with rope. Moving the body is not easy, the plastic is slippery. Braidy with Barbra's help moves the float plane out of the hanger. They have done this before and can manage between the two of them. Braidy gets a four-wheel dolly the mechanics use for moving engines and other heavy parts with. There is a piece of ply-wood that can be placed on the top to keep parts from falling between the frame. Barbra is strong and she and Braidy move the corpse out of the old truck and onto the dolly. They roll the body over to the plane and slide it into the cargo door. There is a big sliding door on the right side of the aircraft for larger items. Braidy isn't hungry even though he hasn't eaten yet this day. Barbra is asking if they need to tie this bad boy down? Braidy doesn't think so, they're not flying far and can take it easy. Besides where can that bad boy goes only on our laps. Barbra tells Braidy that she will fly, she wants to practice landing on the water. Braidy agrees, he has confidence in his student and takes the right-hand seat.

Barbra lines up on the runway and off they go. She rotates smoothly and the old plane pulls its way into a partly cloudy sky. The flight takes only 35 minutes and Barbra slides the plane onto the water. She is trying to keep their arrival quiet, not wanting to alert the village people. She taxi's the plane up to the dock and Braidy ties then up. Barbra climbs out and over to the boathouse. She opens the doors and looks at Braidy with a question,

"hey man, can't we use the runabout instead?"

Braidy looks at the smaller boat and thinks good, why not. Moving the bundle off the smaller boat will be easier and the smaller boat can travel much faster. Barbra untied her boat and idols out and over to the plane. She brings it beside the plane's cargo door and secures the two craft together. She and Braidy slide the dead guy out of the plane and on to the boat. The job isn't so bad, Barbra is strong and Braidy is impressed, she doesn't mind touching corpse's not like Braidy. He is glad they wrapped Melvin up so well, the cover makes it seem less personal.

Barbra takes the controls and Braidy unties them, she backs away turns and then hits the throttle. The inboard outboard isn't as fast as some boats but plenty fast enough. She gets it up on plane and they are skimming over the waves. She knows a spot she is heading for and Braidy is only a passenger, well besides Melvin that is. Barbra has her GPS and is watching the coordinates'. She slows than stops the boat and declares that they have arrived. The spot looks like any other and Braidy looks at her with a question.

"this be the place man, soon you'll see why."

Barbra brings out a knife and cuts the rope binding the bundle. The dead guy is still dead and doesn't complain about the ride. They roll it off the boat and into the water. Barbra has used her knife and opens the corpse's belly cavity. When Melvin hits the water, there is a swirl and sharks grab on the body and begin feasting. Braidy shudders at the sight and moves to the other end of the boat. Barbra is fascinated and watches the destruction with detached interest. She has seen this sight before and knew the spot was just right for eliminating extra dead bodies. Braidy has to wonder at his new friend, he thinks she is being ghoulish. Barba looks back at him and looks sympathetic. She moves over to him, and tells him that it is nature's way, there's nothing personal with sharks. We just brought them lunch or I guess I mean breakfast. Braidy has to agree with her, it looks like there won't be anything left of pore Melvin. Barbra says they can leave, the sharks will clean up everything, they are that hungry.

CHAPTER 25

Mr. Nice cleans up even more, he has his phony documents that look oh so real. He has a badge in a leather holder, and he finds a Crown Vick in the collection of Cars that belonged to the repair shop. The Cars are parked at a nearby parking lot and didn't go up with the building and the three dead dummies. There are 10 or 12 vehicles that he can use he isn't sure if they all run or not, he does know that the Ford does. He drives slowly over to the docks and after he parks, he walks up the boarding ramp. The hired guards are back, watching the ship for Roses company. Soon the ship will be allowed to be unloaded. He needs to retrieve the hidden box in the container now. The guards don't really care, it's not their ship after all. They barely look at his documents and ignore the fancy badge. Mr. Nice is disappointed; he has done such a good job with the badge. He tells the guards that he needs to have some privacy inside the container. No one thinks that's unusual at all, after all he works for the government. He pulls the doors mostly shut and lifts up the ply wood over the metal box hidden in the floor. The box is fastened with long screws into the frame of the container. He has a battery powered screw driver with a special bit that fits the special screws. The screws are used by authorities when something is not supposed to be unscrewed by the general public. The screws aren't hard to get and more Common than everyone believes. The screws Come out with ease using the screw driver and he collects them up and keeps them in his pocket. He doesn't think he will use them again; he just doesn't want anyone to use them as evidence. Mr. Nice lifts out the box, he grunts with the effort. The box is 50 pounds, but he has gotten fat and lazy of late. He has a Cover that he brings out from a small tool box he has brought along and Covers the metal box. The Cover will keep the nosy types from ever seeing the actual box, just a Canvas Covered square object. Mr. Nice is puffing when he arrives at the Ford and has to rest against the fender. He really needs to walk some more or do something to get in better shape.

    Mr. Nice drives off toward another hide-out. He thinks what a stupid name for an apartment, what makes a house a hide-out. Oh well, he is hungry after his big expenditure of energy and stops at an Arby's restaurant for lunch He gets the special five sandwiches for $7 and has a Jamoka too He will start on his new diet tomorrow.

CHAPTER 26

Braidy and Barbra are feeling terrified about dumping Melvin out at sea for a shark's buffet. Braidy didn't have a problem with eliminating the other bad guys, but Melvin is different. Barbra tells him that's ok, she Can keep a secret and has many other ones she knows. Braidy looks at this unusual woman with admiration, she is so full of life. Barbra touches his Cheek so gently that Braidy shivers. He has never known a woman who cared for him so much. He has always been shy and has limited experience with the fare sex. Braidy and Barbra boat back to the island, and Barbra invites him into her house, she fixes them breakfast. Braidy doesn't think he is hungry but when she gets Coffee going, bacon frying and eggs scrambling he discovers he is hungry. She has some rolls she warms in the oven and the smell is heavenly. Braidy watches her moving around the kitchen just waiting and looking and thinks so this is what I've been missing for all my life. He decides to just give her a hug and sneaks up behind her and wraps his long arms around her middle. Barbra is so surprise she drops her spatula, she is quick and relaxes into him She enjoys the feel of this tall vital man and loves his Cent, strength and gentleness. Braidy kisses her neck and takes in her woman Cent and a little ocean smell too. The ocean smell isn't bad at all, she is what she is, she works on the water. Braidy tells her that she is something else.

"and what would that something else be Mr. Braidy sir!"

Braidy doesn't know what to say and just pulls her closer.

"oh yeah, now I understand Mr. Braidy, and that's me too."

Barbra and Braidy call Rose and she says they will need to fly off to Georgia soonest. Braidy doesn't wonder why any more, he tells Barbra he needs to go to work. She tells him she has a charter and will go to the dock on the mainland to meet her new clients. She tells him she will be extra Careful and don't worry. Braidy will worry anyway, it's the way he is, he doesn't worry about himself. They walk over to the dock together, and he helps her bring out the cabin cruiser turned fishing boat. She doesn't need any help of course they are delaying parting is all. Braidy climbs aboard the float plane and she pushes him out with a long pole. He starts engines letting them warm then turns the plane out towards the open sea. He looks back once and she is standing on the dock watching. She waves and he waves back then he is off roaring over the waves and lifting into the sky.

By the time Braidy arrives at the hanger, Ben and Mac are there preparing a King Air, they are just finishing fueling and are ready to help with the float plane. Mac knows nothing about the night before and the early morning flight. He tells Braidy that he is out early. Braidy after stepping down from his plane tells Mac that he misses flying the old plane. He likes to land on the water and of Course is instructing that island girl.

Mac, brushing back his ragged old cap, "so, old man, you say all you do is fly?"

Braidy turns red like the paint jobs on the older equipment. Ben looks the other way; he knows what Barbra and Braidy have been up to. Mac is having fun with Braidy and Ben is asking where Braidy is off to with the big plane? Braidy tells him he thinks Georgia probably to a saw mill or timber Camp. He is waiting for someone from headquarters building to Come out. Mac wipes some grease off the Cowling before Ben or Braidy notices. He wonders how did that grease get there? Mac is the mechanic who last inspected the engines on this aircraft.

Joe drives up, and there is Carmen pretty as a picture stepping out of a new blue over blue van. She whips out her cane like it is a sword and wishes everyone standing around a warm and hardy,

"good good morning boys, are you all waiting for little oh me?"

Braidy is delighted, he enjoys spending time flying with Carmen. He says,

"I'm here Carmen ready, willing, and mostly able to fly you on my magic Carpet anywhere your heart desires."

"well alright, that's more like it, and you know where we are flying off to today?"

Braidy tells her that he doesn't really know but his GPS does. Carmen Comes over to the group using Brady's voice to tell her where they are. She looks like she knows exactly where she is going and the boys are impressed. They aren't surprised with her abilities to travel independently but rather with her blossoming beauty. Carmen has gotten more feminine and beautiful as she has gotten older. She looks like the very pretty woman she is. She walks with gliding steps that seems like she is floating slightly above the ground and holds her shoulders up straight allowing her figure to show to her best advantage. Braidy knows Carmen and says extra words to give her verbal Clues indicating where he is standing. Carmen walks right up to him and takes his big hand. She says,

"hello Mr. Braidy, would you take me flying today?"

"I would be delighted to take you anywhere you would like to go; your slightest wish is my greatest Command."

The boys are always ready for a laugh and they do when they hear those two.

Braidy and Carmen climb aboard the King Air and Carmen takes the right-hand seat and waits for Braidy. He is walking all around the plane looking everything over, although the mechanics have done the same thing. Finally, he enters the plane and sits beside Carmen. He goes down the checklist and starts the engines. The engines have been running before he got there and don't need much warming. He taxis over to the runway and asks if she is ready, yup. Off they go gaining speed as they move along, and after some 2000 feet they lift up into a cloudy sky.

Carmen has a lap top computer she is using with earphones and so can't talk with Braidy. He wants to talk with her about Barbra, nothing personal but how nice she is. Carmen has lists of figures with labels beside them indicating expenditures for the past year. She has had a request for a new log saw. The saw Can whip logs into planks and is precise with its own Computer system. The Camp wants to purchase new logging equipment that will allow them to harvest timber more efficiently. Carmen wants to find out for herself if the equipment is really necessary. She will allow the equipment to be purchased, she just needs to know herself. She has talked with the loggers by phone and has approved smaller equipment but for the expensive saws she needs to be sure. Braidy flies along thinking of Barbra and what they had to do with Melvin's remains. Melvin shouldn't have ever hit Nancy like that, she reacted like the fighter she has become. She trains to defend herself and others and when she or the people she is protecting are in danger she fights back. She didn't even think about shooting Melvin, she defended herself with the weapon at hand. Melvin was a fool for striking an armed woman who is a trained killer. Braidy doesn't know what will happen when the authorities hear Barbra's story but the paper work looked ok, so maybe it will be alright. Braidy doesn't even know if he will be involved if there is an investigation. The best thing to do is just keep quiet and say nothing to anyone.

The new King Airs are so nice to fly, they are quiet and faster. He Cannot leave the flight deck; Carmen can't fly the plane. She Can go back and get him something to munch on though. When Carmen pulls off her earphones, he asks her,

"hey Carmen dear?"

She finishes for him,

"say Braidy, may I get something for you to eat?"

"I thought you would never ask, and yes thank you, you're so sweet."

"I hope you're not thinking of having me for a snack buster."

He tells her no, she's not in any danger, he just Can't leave the flight deck. She unbuckles and stands up and moves back to the refreshment Center. They Call it a refreshment Center, it's just a counter top with a micro-wave and a small refrigerator. Theirs a sink and some cupboards and Carmen builds Braidy a giant sandwich that would last her all day but will only last Braidy for a few hours. Boy what must it be like to be hungry almost all the time, he is so skinny too. She finds a Cold drink and rips off some paper towels and brings her friend some fuel

Barbra reports the missing Melvin to the police. They have instigated a search party and the Coast Guard are looking too. She directs them to an area of the ocean miles from the actual spot. They look all day the first and the next but no Melvin. Barbra is a good actor; she is resourceful and even sheds a tear. She even helps in the search joining in with everyone else. They give up and Call it an accident and no one complains, there are more than 300 drownings every year off the Coast of Washington. Barbra visits with Rose and reassures her that it's alright. Rose likes this woman admiring her tenacity and energy. Barbra wares her usual Cargo shorts with a mostly Clean shirt. She has had shirts made up with a giant fish a Crossed the front and the name of her Company beneath. She is proud of what she has been able to do practically from nothing and of Course lots of luck. Rose offers Barbra some money for her trouble and Barbra tells Rose no thanks. She doesn't need money she says,

"excuse me Ms. Rose, Can you be telling me when that man Braidy is coming back?"

Rose has heard that there may be a blooming romance in the works and tells her tomorrow. She asks Barbra if she would like to stay for lunch? Barbra has forgotten about eating since breakfast the day before and decides that she must be hungry. She accepts Roses invitation and goes over to admire Nancy's baby, and says hello to Nancy too. Jones and Nancy are going over the events in Los Angeles and Jack is apparently babysitting. He lays beside Nance's play pen and looks over at the baby. Jack is healing up and will get the stitches out later today. He has his Chin on his paws and is about one foot away from the baby. Nance gazes in wonder at Jacks giant nose so Close. Jack doesn't move and is fascinated with this very special little girl. Nancy and Jones are going through books of pictures of various bad guys, Jones doesn't know ware Nancy has gotten all the photos and doesn't ask. Nancy has hundreds in books and loose pages she puts back into folders. Jones doesn't recognize anyone in the pictures and Nancy sighs, no picture means no identification. Nancy asks if Joe Can come up to the office for a minute? Joe is good at drawing people from someone's description and she decides to give it a try. Joe Comes in the office Carrying a large pad of drawing paper and a box of pencils. He lays out his supplies on the table and says to Jones, "just close your eyes and try and recall any thing about this guy, anything at all of what he looked like. If you can't remember, then think of the particulars that aren't like the guy. Jones looks at Joe like he has two heads,

"what do you mean, the things that aren't like him?"

"you know, opposite what you're sure he is not."

Jones thinks he may start drinking soon, he doesn't get it. Nancy laughs at Jones and says,

"ask yourself if the dude was fat or skinny or in between."

"Right, was he black or white or some ware in the middle Joe asks."

Jones doesn't need that bull, he does remember what Mr. Nice looked like and even the finger nail polish. Joe picks up a number 2 pencil testing the point and licking the tip. He makes a few curves on the page filling in as Jones remembers and, in a few minutes, there is a drawing of Mr. Nice. Jones,

"Holy shit, that's him, how did you do that?"

Joe shrugs and wants to add more details, hair Color, eye Color, any distinguishing tattoos or scars? Jones is impressed and thinks about it more. Jones says,

"that's all for now, I see what your trying to do, and will think about any details I may have missed.

Rose and Joni Come up with lunch, they have gone around the Corner to the deli for Corn beef on rye and the works. Jones loves corn beef on rye and especially the huge dill pickles that Come with each sandwich. Barbra is loving Roses coffee and has had three cups already. She likes good coffee, having her own but this coffee is better. Rose says it's the way it is ground don't you know. Barbra doesn't understand how grinding beans could make any difference in how coffee tastes. Rose is kidding of Course it doesn't make any difference how Coffee is ground. The coffee her father favored is blended specifically for the Company and is actually several different kinds of beans from several countries. The lunch is spread out on the new table and since little Nance is fast asleep and Jack is babysitting, they leave Nance in good paws. Jack wants to help with lunch but is a good mutt and stays with the baby.

Barbra doesn't know if she should talk about the early morning sea voyage with Braidy, from several days ago, she doesn't know if all the people know what happened or not and decides to say nothing. She and Rose have talked some but need to say more. Barbra is cheery and enjoys the meal immensely. The chips are oven baked and aren't greasy. The rye bread is fresh, they baked their own and the Corn beef isn't stringy. The mustard is creamy and rich and the dill pickles are puckeringly delicious. The coffee goes good with anything but really good with corn beef on rye.

CHAPTER 27

Braidy and Carmen land at Atlanta international airport and rent a car. Braidy knows the way to the camp and tells Carmen she doesn't need her GPS app. She doesn't listen and calls up the app. She says she likes to practice just in case Braidy gets lost. Braidy stops at Burger King and orders up a big bag of burgers. Carmen gets a small milk shake, chocolate of course. She keeps it small; she is afraid she is getting too fat. Braidy thinks she is just right; everything is ware it is supposed to be. Carmen is still slurping when Braidy was up the wrappers from lunch and drives them out to the logging camp. The camp is neat and clean, the buildings look well-kept and there are no weeds or brush encroaching on buildings. Braidy and Jones came here a year or so ago and broke up a KKK gang of prejudice bad guys. The entire team of loggers have been replaced with an all-black crew. The boss guy is a Mary round man who looks like a black Santa Clause. He isn't really fat, but just looks that way. He rolls over to the rental Car and offers his hand to Braidy. He remembers Braidy from before, he is the one who hired him. His name as Braidy recalls is Carson. Carson doesn't know Carmen, he has talked to her only on the phone. She gets out on her side and whips out her folding cane. She uses a folding cane when traveling so the cane takes up less space. She also doesn't want anyone to move her cane without telling her. She has been stranded when some well-meaning sighted person stood her straight Cane up in a Corner without telling her. She needs her Cane but it is gone and she has no idea where it may be. So, she uses a folding Cane that she Can store in her pocket or purse out of sight out of mind.

Carson is quite a lady's man, he his expansive and offers Carmen his hand too. She doesn't miss a beat, she offers her small hand and says,

"hello Mr. Carson, I'm your boss so to speak." "Braidy and I will decide if you are worthy of possessing a new million dollars saw or not. Carson steps back a half step and looks for help from his men. They know nothing and admire the trees and all. Carmen isn't Cruel and smiles big as all outdoors and says,

"Mr. Carson I'm always such a kidder it will be alright, show me what you got please."

Carson then sees she is holding a white Cane and looks to Braidy for an answer. Braidy mentions that Carmen is blind but don't let that fool him, she's the best and doesn't miss a thing. Carson isn't stupid and Catches on, and tells Carmen to follow him. Carmen Comes around the Car and takes Brady's arm, he has been a human guide for her before. They walk over to the machine shed ware they equipment is stored and repaired. The pieces of the broken saw are laid out on the Cement floor.

Braidy moving his cap to the back of his big block head says, "we didn't know that the saw was broken, when did this happen?"

Carson tells them that it just happened earlier this morning. We brought most of the pieces here to try and fix everything, the welds have busted loose and will take lots of fixing. We have to grind out the old weld before re-welding, and the new weld has to be perfect. There is a lot of strain on the joint there. And of Course, none of us is really that good a welder. Braidy looks it over explaining to Carmen as he looks. She doesn't know much about machinery but has been around enough to understand that this saw is finished. Carmen stops Brady's narration before he gets half way around and tells Carson she will get them a new saw. He Can't work with this antiquated equipment. Production has been good up till now and Rose and she are satisfied with his team's work. Carson is relieved and invites them in for some Coffee and maybe some of Cookies fresh sweet rolls. Braidy looks up at that, and says,

"now you're talking."

"how Can you be hungry, after burger King and the giant sandwich earlier?"

"well you see I'm a growing boy, and need to keep up my strength."

Carson says to Carmen,

"I have a granny who is blind, and she takes my arm sometimes when I take her to Church.

Carmen has heard this kind of thing often, and is gracious to him. She says to Carson,

"why thank you Mr. Carson that's very thoughtful of you, and besides Braidy walks like a giant. Carson looks at Braidy than back at Carmen and says,

"that Braidy man is at least 18 inches taller than you, and it's no wonder he walks bigger. She has never had it put quite that way before, and takes his strong arm. The arm is hard muscle and she admires his strength. Carson is warm and friendly to Carmen and tells her all about the Camp and its few troubles. Carmen isn't dumb, she knows that men often will tell a blind girl more than they want to. In this Case it's nothing she is alarmed about. Carson says they have visited other Camps, one in South Carolina, and he says,

"they got an elephant, a giraffe and what was that other Critter? Oh yeah, a Camel. Carmen knows all about the Circus animals but pretends like she doesn't. She says,

"do you mean a real live elephant?"

Carson goes on to tell her that they use that big elephant for moving huge logs around, and she works for practically nothing. Carmen tells him that that elephants name is Rose. Carson says to her, isn't that the bosses name too? Carmen tells him yes that's right.

Braidy is looking the broken machinery over Carefully and says to Carmen

"this equipment Can't be used any more, and even if Carson here and his gang Can weld it back together it is very dangerous. Carmen agrees and turns to Carson,

"Mr. Carson, we will purchase new equipment for you guys, I am sorry for the extra trouble, my job is to make sure everyone is safe and that the production doesn't stop."

Carson is impressed by this young lady, and she does her job in spite of her obvious blindness. He wonders if he Could do work if he were suddenly blind like her. Carmen asks,

"Mr. Carson sir, have you decided on what brand of replacement equipment you would like?"

He tells Carmen that they have the one they think is the best selected, and by the way, she Can Call him just plane Carson. Carmen says,

"ok Mr. Just Plane Carson sir, let's get this show on the road please, how do we Contact the manufacturer and when Can the equipment be delivered? Carson,

The equipment is made in Vermont and will take three days to deliver than two or three to set up. Since we don't have a big enough powerline to deliver electricity for the new equipment, we will have to get one with a Diesel engine or maybe Propane Carmen knows that electric is the most efficient and asks,

"why Can't they install more powerlines for you?"

"well mam, I'm not sure of Course, when one of us asks the management are always too busy to discuss the reason.

"bull shit, oops, sorry about that, I need to be a lady, right!"

Carmen being a lady doesn't seem to matter with this bunch, they howl with laughter and gather around Carmen and tell her she's alright. Carmen is warmed by their acceptance and puts up her small hand for hi-fives. They are gentle with her small and delicate hand, they have Callas upon Callas on their big paws. Braidy has been watching and Comes over to Carmen,

"We Can visit the electricity people and you Can work your magic on them, and I'll bet lunch that these gentlemen will have Current soon. Carmen asks ware the office is that serves this area with electric power. Carson tells them, and Carmen says to him give me a few hours before ordering the new equipment. Carson, bowing,

"yes mam, and thank you."

Carson invites them to the dining hall for Coffee and some fresh baked rolls. Carmen doesn't get a Chance to answer, Braidy takes her hand and says

"yes, now you're talking."

Carson waves his arm toward the log structure they use for dining and they all troop over for some Coffee and goodies. Braidy smiles at the sight of fresh baked rolls and brewing Coffee and Carmen is placed at the head of the table in the place of honor.

CHAPTER 28

Braidy and Carmen drive off to the local utility's office. They find the building alright and are told to wait, and after an hour finally they are directed into an office. The man sitting behind the desk is a small guy and is not friendly. He is bothered by their visit, he is a very busy man, and has a lot to do. Carmen knows she is in for difficult time, and uses her best Charm. Her Charm isn't working, this guy is extremely prejudice against any one different and especially anyone who is blind. Braidy isn't about to take any Crap from this little squirt and stands up his full Hight. The boss guy has to look up to see his face, and shudders some. He tells them that he will Call the police with any sign of trouble. Braidy tells him that they have a bunch of lawyers that will Cause him more trouble than he wants. The guy isn't affected and asks him to sit down. Carmen stands up also, she is only five foot tall and he looks at her rather than Braidy. Carmen is trim and looks pretty, she uses a brilliant smile and even this old fart is impressed finally. She says,

"I'm very sorry sir, I didn't get your name, I'm Carmen I'm glad to meet you, holding out her very lovely hand."

The old fart, holds out his hand without thinking about it and says he is Wendel Miles She takes his hand with both her small ones and gently squeezes. Mr. Miles Can't help but react and respond with a slight smile. Carmen is smiling big as Christmas and says,

"Mr. Miles, allow us to introduce ourselves properly, this is Mr. Braidy and we are from the Company that owns the logging Camp west of town."

Miles doesn't like black folks, and wants to say that but doesn't, he has Come under Carmen's delicate Charm. He tells them to please have a seat, and would you like anything to drink? Braidy just loves to watch Carmen working, he slides his Chair back away from the front of Miles's desk. He knows that this is all about Carmen taking Charge and will keep mostly still. Carmen thanks him for the offer and sits back down moving her Chair slightly Closer. She is Confining almost like she and Miles have a secret between them. She tells him that they will need a bigger powerline out to the Camp for some new equipment. She is authorized to help with the expenses, and Miles is surprised at that. Carmen has just thought of it and doesn't know if she has that authority or not. She knows Rose and believes that it will be ok. Miles tells her the poles, wires, and labor Come to $3000 per mile, and it's at least 20 miles. Carmen isn't put off by that, she knows how much it will really Cost, and says that she Can pay for the new poles and wire if his Company Can provide the labor. Mr. Miles perks up at that and readily agrees. And just like that, the Camp will have the Current they need for the new equipment. Braidy and Carmen are off, leaving Mr. Miles actually almost grinning. They have negotiated like this before in other situations and are satisfied Carmen doesn't take Brady's arm; she wants to show these prejudice rebels that she is an independent woman. Braidy knows how she feels and walks behind her and is ready for quiet words if she needs help. She has a good memory and he isn't needed. When they get back in the rental Car Braidy asks,

"I don't mean to be a wet blanket, but where are we going to get 20 miles worth of poles and wire. Carmen doesn't know, she tells him to have faith, they will find that stuff some ware, she hopes.

When they arrive back at the logging Camp the Crew is nervous and don't want to talk much. Carmen senses the worry and finds Carson,

"She takes his big hand and asks him what's the matter?"

Carson tells her that they have heard from the Camp in South Carolina, and that Rosy the elephant has been shot, she isn't going to make it they say. Carmen is shocked and gasps, she turns to Braidy asking,

"How far is it to the Camp in South Carolina?"

Braidy tells her they Can fly over to that airport in less than an hour and will have to rent a Car unless someone Can meet them at the airport. Carmen takes his arm and says,

"yes, please Can we go there?"

Carmen tells Carson that they will get them the electricity they need and to go ahead and order the equipment using electrical power. She and Braidy move over to the rental and drive to the airport. Braidy knows his friend and drives fast. They leave the rental car in the airport parking and get quickly to the airplane. Carmen doesn't even ask; she pulls out the wheel-chalks and stores them away. Braidy unlocks the plane and gets going with pre-start check list. Carmen is close to tears thinking about the elephant she knows she is so sentimental about all kinds of things but especially animals. She wishes that Jack were here to provide Jack support. Carmen uses her satellite phone and Calls the South Carolina camp. Cookie answers the phone in the dining room.

"hi Cookie, this is Carmen from headquarters, do you remember me?"

Cookie does and is glad to hear from her, and asks if she knows about their elephant? Carmen tells him that's why she is calling. She asks if there is any change? Cookie says that there is no change, they have called a vet but she says there's nothing she can do. The bullet was a large caliber maybe from an elephant gun. The bullet struck Rosy in the chest and her lungs are filling up with blood. Carmen starts to cry but stops herself knowing she needs to be strong. She tells Cookie they are flying over from Atlanta and could someone meet them at the airport to save time. Cookie says yes of course he will come right away and meet them where they park the plane.

When Carmen and Braidy arrive at camp with Cookie, they are driven out to ware Rosy is laying. All the loggers are standing around and looking sad and some are looking really mad. They want to get their guns and track down the bastard that shot their Rosy. They have all become attached to this grate beast and will miss her. Carmen wants to touch Rosy and finds her way over to her. The vet is a young woman not much taller than Carmen and is caring, she offers Carmen her hand. Carmen recognizes a fellow animal lover and takes her offered hand. Carmen,

"Hello doctor, I'm Carmen from the head office, is there anything you need that I Can get for you?"

The vet says her name is Janet, and adds, "unfortunately, there aren't any trauma Centers for elephants around here, I Can try something surgical maybe. The bullet is still in there, and if I can cauterize the bleeders maybe she could have a chance. The pore thing is drowning in her own blood. Carmen tells her that anything is ok, and if she wants to try, she can. She turns to the gathering of men and asks if that would be alright? They know this young woman from previous visits and know she will do everything possible to help. Carmen tells Janet yes please try and let her know what she needs. Janet tells her that she isn't sure of what she is doing, she has never worked on an elephant before. Janet tells them she will need a method to cauterize the bleeders when she gets to the damaged parts. The men are thinking about that wondering how to create enough heat out here from power sources to burn the tissues. They all look at the trucks, and start to gather wire and metal and decide to give it their best try. Janet says,

"this isn't the best Circumstances you know; I might kill this pore girl myself."

Carmen asks her if she will try? Janet sees the Concern and Compassion on Carmen's face and just has to try.

CHAPTER 29

Rose isn't ready to hear any worse news especially about that elephant. She likes animals sure, but that elephant has been a royal pain in the, well it's not lady like to say ware. She has gotten some large bills for the Critters Care, lots of hay when the trees weren't enough. Why would a lumber company need to buy 45 tons of hay? Rose sighs to herself and says to go ahead do what they can for Rosy the elephant. Jones is listening and wonders why anyone would want to kill Rosy the elephant for what reason? Jones knows about large animals, thinking of his cows back on the dairy farm in Nebraska. In all his years of raising animals and milking cows he has never had to deal with gunshot wounds, Jones pets Jacks big head and looks at his Rose. She is pacing again, something she has been doing lately when she is troubled. He knows better than to interrupt her and just waits with Jack for her to decide. Rose doesn't want to think about elephants however, two of her biggest ships need new Captains, the Rose Marie, and the ship named after her father. She thinks she will have that ships name changed. She looks at Jones and asks him,

"Mr. Jones, how would you like to have a ship named after you?"

Jones looks back at her and says,

"well I guess that would be nice, but maybe you will tell me what this is all about, I Can see you're troubled, you are wearing out the Carpet."

Rose looks down at the Carpet she has been treading on for so long and it does look more warn than the surrounding carpet. She Comes over to him and makes a place for herself on his lap and snuggles in for a Cozy sit. Jones holds her close enjoying the feel and Cent of this so very special woman. She says, we need two new Captains and some experienced engine room guys also. The new ships don't need as many Crew as the older ships but the real problem is, the machinery is much more Complex. Jones nibbles her ear, and she says,

"stop that, how Can I think if you are having me for lunch?"

Jones reminds her that lunch time was hours ago, now it's time for high-tea. She smiles at her man and then starts to giggle. Jack sigh's, and wanders over toward the small kitchen just in case something got dropped by his wonderful friend Braidy.

CHAPTER 30

Barbra knows nothing of the troubles in Roses Company, she has troubles of her own. She has been guiding guys out on the ocean and helping them catch some impressive fish. She likes her job and some of the same men Come back for more. Usually they bring friends along and that's good for business. Barbra has collected four guys this time and is chugging over to a favorite spot when the engine just stops. The Diesel has frozen up, and when she tries the starter theirs only a clunk. She doesn't know as much about engines as she needs to and thinks she will call for help. She calls her village friends and asks them if they can come out with the runabout and rescue everyone. One of the women agrees and says she will walk over and get the runabout. Barbra tells her ware the spare key is hidden.

She looks at her guest, "I be sorry gentlemen, my engine here just quit on me, and we will have to use my other boat."

The men are not happy and say so.

"we Can fish right here, it's Close enough to ware I was taking you anyway. The four shrug and pick up their fishing poles and Caste the loaded hooks out over the water. Right away one has a strike and he knows that he has something big on the line. Barbra watches the line and something doesn't look like a fish, it isn't jerking and pulling like fish do. When the catch gets closer, she is horrified to see that it's a body, most gone but still recognizable as human. The man looks at the body than at her, and bends over and throws up Coffee Danish oat meal and bacon from breakfast. Barbra is afraid too; she is wondering if this body could be what's left of that Melvin fellow. The body has missing legs and arms, but the torso and head are mostly there. She can't tell, maybe this guy used to be a black man mostly by the shape of the eye sockets and Lord forgive her the remaining teeth. The teeth are bright and white and look enormous in the jaws. She is probably wrong, she can't really tell for sure, she has been feeling funny about Brady's early morning visit a few weeks ago, she is good, and says they will need to contact the police. The four fishermen don't want to fish anymore and put away their poles. They go inside the cabin and sit down to wait. Barbra looks the body over and decides that she Can't tell what color this pore fellow use to be. She knows shark bites though and sees that this guy was some sharks lunch for sure. The bite wounds are from a large mouthed fish and nothing makes those kinds of bites other than a shark.

CHAPTER 31

In South Carolina Doctor Janet is using a huge knife sharpened like a razor to Cut through the thick hide of an elephant. At one point, she uses a hand saw, and she gets to the bullet after working harder than she has ever worked before. The elephant is still alive though no one knows why. Carmen is touching the elephant near her ear and talking to her. She thought she may have noticed Rosie's ear move slightly when she was talking to her but Can't be sure. She talks with a gentle voice that she has used with Jack when he was shot and maybe her presents is helping. The procedure isn't pretty, its bloody and messy. Doctor Janet isn't a large woman or particularly strong but hangs in there. She hands the bloody bullet to Braidy who finds a tissue that's Clean in his pocket. He doesn't know what they will do with this evidence but decides it's the thing to do. Rosy is still breathing but slowly. Doctor Janet doesn't know if that's good or bad, elephants aren't her specialty. The device the guys have rigged up for Cauterizing Rosie's wounds makes the flesh smoke and the elephant move slightly at each application. The bleeding is slowing and many leaks have stopped. Dr. Janet doesn't have any idea how she will Close up the huge Cut she has had to make. She looks at the guys with a question. They don't know, and just look back at her. Carmen asks what's going on now, what's the matter? Doctor Janet tells her that they don't have a way of sewing up the wound. Carmen is thinking that over. She asks if the guys have antibiotics in medicine kits? They allow they do and one offers to go after all they have back at Camp. He drives off in one of the trucks. Everyone from Camp is there, they all love this big elephant and are worried. Doctor Janet tries to pull the wound together with her small hands and is only partly successful the guys see what she is trying to do and offer to help. The men have strong hands and two guys Can push the wound together from both sides. The wound doesn't look so bad Closed up and she wishes she Could sew the wound together just like that. One guy Called Harry says,

"what about using a Cordless drill and drilling small holes through that tough hide than using some of that heavy Cord we use for tying up boxes with, you know when we have to ship something heavy. Dr. Janet looks at the elephants hide and does wonder how she will ever get any kind of needle into and out of that thick hide. Another guy roars off in a truck to Camp; to get a drill and some Cord. The first guy Comes back with all the anti-biotic they have and offers it to the doctor. He has at least a dozen tubes and they have not been opened before. Dr. Janet lets the wound come open slightly, she is telling the two helpers to let the wound open just enough to get the medicine in. She squeezes one tube after another getting the gooey stuff all over the outside too. She is a mess with antibiotic all over her Clothes and hands and some in her hair. The second guy Comes back with a drill, the Cord, needle nose plyers, drill bits and an all. Braidy thinks that this boy is ok, thinking of practically everything. They all shudder when they see the Doctor drilling holes in the elephant with a cordless drill, she drills two holes on both sides of the wound then pushes the Cord through the openings. She gets all the holes drilled first than begins to gently pull the wound together. The job is done and looks like a mad seamstress has had a fun day. The elephant is still breathing that surprises everyone. Carmen is still talking in her ear; she has been bending Close to rosie's ear the entire time. They are all surprised that it is nearly dark, they have been here for 5 hours. Braidy is standing there with all the rest and asks,

"is their anyway to move this girl some ware more Comfortable?"

We Could use one of the big cats and drag her to the camp but that wouldn't be so good for the elephant. Dr. Janet says,

"This is as good a place as anywhere else, we can watch her here. Carmen,

"Dr. Janet, thank you for all that you are doing, you worked really hard, and I'm grateful."

Janet looks down at herself, she is a mess, elephant blood all over her, in her hair, and all over her genes and shirt, even on her shoes. She tells Carmen,

"you're welcome, let's just hope we helped this pore girl, we just have to wait now, the rest is up to Rosy here."

CHAPTER 32

Barbra's friends from the village arrive in the runabout and everyone goes aboard, the four men aren't looking quite as green and will have some tall tales to tell their friends. Barbra will have to stay with her big boat, she needs to be available when the Coast guard arrive bringing the local cops. She doesn't think that anyone Can identify the corpse as anyone, it's just a Chunk of what used to be human maybe. The body has been pulled in close to her boat and she doesn't like it being so close. She isn't afraid of death; she just doesn't want the thing being so close if it is Melvin's remains.

The coast Guard arrive after forever and take one look at the dead guy and look away. They will have to retrieve the remains from the water and aren't looking forward to that at all. Barbra knows these guys and has kidded with them at various times. They aren't kidding now, and look at her with pity. She doesn't need this for her business, word gets around. Barbra isn't concerned about her business, she will Mary Braidy and work with him for that big company. She misses her man and is wondering where he is and what he is doing. She says she will pull the Corpse over to the Coast Guard boat for them, she has a pole with a hook on the end. She doesn't worry about the corpse as a dead person, but only if it might be what's left of that Melvin fellow. She moves the body over to the other boat and pulls it on board. The body isn't very heavy, and she maneuvers it into a body bag that one Guardsman holds open for her. They close the bag shut and everyone feels better, the remains are out of sight. The Coasties offers Barbra a toe back to her island and she accepts gladly. She was wondering how she would do that, and they offer her a solution. Barbra ties up her broken boat and wearily walks over to her house. She has removed all the furniture that the bad guys have destroyed and the house looks empty. She has moved some lawn furniture into the Livingroom and sits on outdoor furniture inside the house. Barbra is feeling so sad and just has to call that office and find out what's happening with her man. When she calls, Joni answers even though it's getting late, Barbra asks about Braidy, and then asks for Rose. Barbra tells Rose about Catching Melvin's remains maybe, but don't worry none, that corpse don't look like anything or anyone. She tells Rose it will be ok, the corpse if it is Melvin has already been identified as Melvin and if sharks got him some more what does it matter Rose has to agree with that and thinks it will be ok, and she asks,

"would you like to Come over for dinner and to talk?"

Barbra thinks why not, she notices that her runabout was left tied up to the dock. Those village people are so nice, and thoughtful. She did notice also that the well has been filled in, and if you didn't know where it had been you would never know it was there in the first place. Barbra gets herself Cleaned up, the shower in this big house is large, big enough for her and Mr. Braidy. She looks at herself in the mirror and isn't impressed, she is starting to look her age that is older than most people think. She has always prided herself looking younger than her real age, but after today she's not so sure. She is really 45 years old, and thinks that Braidy being 55 isn't so much difference. She thinks Braidy is so nice and wants him more every day. She will get her man and she will show him what an island girl Can love like.

When she arrives at headquarters building, she is let in by Joni, and they take the elevator to the top floor. Rose, Nancy, Joe, and that grate big dog Jack are admiring Nancy's baby. The baby looks just like Nancy and will be a beauty when she grows up. Barbra has dolled up some and looks nice, the other women admire her and say how nice she looks. Barbra tells them thank you, and is feeling better after they tell her that she Can look like a girl. She is looking all around for that Jones fellow but doesn't want to ask. Rose tells her that Jones had to fly the helicopter down the coast and will be back soon. The women drink coffee and chat about girl talk, Jack lies Close to the baby and joe is finishing the day covering the front desk.

CHAPTER 33

At the logging camp, the loggers, Braidy, Carmen and Doctor Janet are all watching the elephant, all through the night. They have portable work lights set up and a small generator off in the distant supply's electricity for the lights. Rosy doesn't move, she is very Critical. Dr. Janet is wondering if she Could get some fluids into her patient, and mentions that. Carmen whips out her smart phone and uses the internet feature to look up information on elephant intravenous fluid replacement. She finds more than she thought, and tells the doctor,

"it says here that you Can add fluids to an elephant, it's similar to adding fluids you use for Cows. You need somewhere from 100 to 300 liters of fluid for elephants."

The doctor has to think about that one, that's a lot of fluid, and probably she Can't get that much, and what kind of needle would you have to use. She decides to Call a friend at the Atlanta zoo. He's not much of a friend but better than no friend. She wants to know if Carmen Can find numbers on her phone? Carmen tells her of course, what number would she like. Well, she gives out his name, and Carmen starts hunting. Carmen is good as her word and finds someone at the zoo, and hands the phone to Dr. Janet. She isn't sure how to talk about this elephant out in the Carolina woods but just jumps in with both feet. The zoo guy is friendly and says he understands, he had been wondering what ever happened to Rosy the elephant, he wanted the zoo to get her. He says he Can help, and will need some time to get there. Braidy is volunteered by Carmen to fly after him, and goes over to him to lay on the charm. Braidy doesn't need to be charmed, he has been taken in like everyone else and is glad to help in any way he can. Braidy will fly over to Atlanta and bring the zoo vet, and Carmen says she wants to stay with Rosy. Braidy asks to be taken back to camp to drive to the airport in the rental Car.

The elephant watchers have had a long night of it, the guys have brought sleeping bags and started a small fire and so it's like camping out. Dr. Janet goes back to Camp and Cleans up, she grabs a shower in one of the trailer houses used for homes by the loggers and is provided some Coveralls that Come from the smallest logger. The coveralls are still much too large for her and she has to roll up the pant legs and the sleeves. She doesn't complain, and Cookie tells her that he will wash the bloody Clothes for her and will bring them out when they are done. Cookie also brings everyone sandwiches that are made from what would have been last night's roast beef dinner. The sandwiches are delicious as good as any deli food. He brings a big Cake and a big coffee pot that Can be used over the open fire. This guy can really cook, and it's too bad for Braidy he will miss all the goodies. Cookie doesn't forget Braidy and has a paper bag full of good things to eat. Braidy gets to the airport and walks all around the airplane, and settles up with the fuel provider. The company use gold cards that are good anywhere. The bills for fuel get paid by book keeping and no one ever complains but the bills got to be really big. Fuel for the King Airs must be in the thousands for each trip.

The Vet from the zoo is waiting at the airport in Atlanta and so the turnaround time is small. The Doctor has several large boxes that he brings on board, and Braidy after he introduces himself welcomes him aboard and they are off roaring down the runway and lifting into the Georgia sky.

They land in South Carolina and are met by a guy from camp. They drive out to camp and then on to the elephant. Nothing has changed, the elephant is still breathing and Carmen is there by Rosie's ear talking quietly. The doctors greet each other and the zoo vet gets to work. Dr. Janet watches she is fascinated, and when the zoo dock pulls out one giant needle everyone gasps. The needle is very large and hopefully sharp. He gets a vain right away and one of the loggers holds up the fluid above the elephant. They will rig up a way of holding up the fluid containers but now the guys want to help. Liter after liter go in, there are five hundred liters of fluid available and they keep pumping in the stuff. Rosy doesn't move, she lies their piece fully existing. Carmen wants this girl to recover, she has some history with the elephant, and wills her to recover. And finally, after 20 hours she does. The elephant lets out a huge bubble of elephant gas otherwise known as a fart and everyone has to move back. Carmen too moves back about 25 feet closing her nose. Rosy moves her trunk and wants to try and get up. Dr. Janet doesn't want Rosy to move just yet, and says that. Carmen Comes back over and talks in her ear; she is Calming and her soft touch keeps the elephant still. Carmen really does have a way with animals. Rosy recovers fast, the fluids have made all the difference. She is growing stronger by the minute and will be alright. Doctor Janet is so grateful to the zoo doctor. She never does know his name, just the zoo Doctor Braidy has a quick talk with the zoo doctor, he wants the zoo to take Rosy. The camp guys are sad but realized that would be best for the elephant. After all they can visit her whenever they go to Atlanta. The zoo vet arranges transportation for Rosy, the Camel and the two show ponies, and the giraffe, they have a truck they use for moving large animals like elephants. The truck will take a while to arrive, and when it looks like Rosy will be alright, Carmen and Braidy will need to get back to the camp in Georgia

 Carmen and Braidy are really tired and need to rest, they get hotel rooms and check in after some dinner or is it breakfast. They sleep until early afternoon than get back in the rental Car. They arrive at the logging camp about five in the afternoon just Intime for dinner with the camp folks. Carmen isn't hungry but of course good old Braidy is. Carson tells them he has ordered the new equipment and it will be shipped soon Braidy tells him about what happened with the elephant. Carson listens but doesn't know the elephant and is not as affected as everyone else.

 Braidy chomping a huge chunk of meatloaf says, "We will need 20 miles worth of wooden poles for the powerlines, and he will find a supplier for the poles. The poles will probably be from southern pine and creosoted and as for the wire, well he is working on that. Actually, Carmen has been working on that little need, she is researching the internet and their own Company resources for wire. The electricity will be high voltage and when the lines get to the Camp there will be a transformer that will reduce down the power to 440 volts. The new equipment will run on the electricity that Comes from the nearby substation. The initial investment will be somewhat high but soon it will pay off.

Carmen makes the arrangements and she and Braidy Can fly back to Seattle. When they arrive at the hanger, there is a reception Committee waiting for them. Rose and Barbra are there along with little Nance. Nancy is back to work and is following up on some leads. Joe has made a respectable drawing of Mr. Nice. Nancy is talking with a friend in the police department. She is trying to keep the investigation quiet but the contact at the police department says this guy is wanted by several branches of various police services. He tells Nancy that they have been looking for this guy for years. If she knows anything about Mr. Nice, she needs to share that with everyone. Nancy doesn't care, she just wants this bad guy off the streets and away from her company. She has given herself away with Joe's drawing, it is really good and her contact asks "where did you get this drawing, and who provided the details of what he looks like?"

Nancy knows nothing, only that one of the employees got a good look at Mr. Nice just for an instant. The cop is suspicious and doesn't believe her, he has every right to doubt, Nancy is lying big time. She Cannot say how involved she and her people really are. She says,

"I will tell you what I know when I know it, you Can count on me."

Braidy and the guys put away the airplane, and the mechanics don't even rag him about wrecking the plane. The plane is just fine, it's just something that they do for some fun. Carmen wants to hold the baby and Rose hands her over. Carmen tells Rose all about Rosy the elephant and says,

"Rosy dear, you will be glad to know that your name sake will be living in the Atlanta zoo from now on, and I offered a small donation for her care, only one years' worth of hay."

"pore Rose rolls her eyes and says how much?"

Carmen tells her that its only around sixty tuns of hey, not much."

Rose just groans and wonders where Jones is, she hasn't heard from him for a while. She doesn't worry about Jones; he flies as well as Braidy and will be back soon. Just then she hears it before she sees it the helicopter Comes swooping in over the top of the hanger and settles down on the apron. The helicopter is a pretty light blue over a darker blue and is shiny and clean. She loves the look of the new paint job on nearly everything including each piece of equipment. The equipment that isn't painted the new Colors will be sold off or retired.

After Jones shuts down the Jet Ranger he walks over to Rose and picks her up in a giant bear hug. She is used to him but never knows if she will get a tiny kiss or a big hug. Sometimes with these big hugs she becomes airborne, she is lifted off her feet by Jones's enthusiasms

CHAPTER 34

Mr. Nice has to report to people higher up the food Chain. He tries to stay Cool and Cannot. He is used by the big guys and knows it. He doesn't like being used and abused but hasn't any choice, they treat him like a beast of burden. The meeting places are always different, he gets directions by public phones. He waits until the phone rings, gets the info than moves to the next phone. There aren't as many public phones any more, the distances are miles apart. Mr. Nice finally arrives at the meeting place and is searched by big black guys who aren't gentle. They practically turn him upside down and push him around too. Finally, he is allowed into the inter sanction to meet Mr. Big. He doesn't know who Mr. Big is, the guy wares a mask. The masks are always different, and his voice is altered by a little box thing. Mr. Big wants the metal box from the container that had the Chinese women. Mr. Nice says,

"I didn't bring it with me, I will need to get it for you."

"you had better be right, the gentlemen will go with you, and if you're lying, you're dead.

Mr. Nice gulps and gets up to leave. Mr. Big,

"wait a minute, I'm not finished yet, you will do more if you survive the killing."

For some reason the last Comment makes Mr. Big roar with laughter, the laughter sounds hideous and not natural. Mr. Nice is shaking in his shoes, he looks away. Today's mask is Richard Nixon and is ugly.

Mr. Nice takes the folded paper one of Mr. Biggs bad boys offers. Mr. Nice has had these kinds of papers before and is relieved not to have to hear Mr. Biggs voice any longer than he has to. Mr.

Nice looks back at Mr. Big, he simply waves him away, like shooing away flies.

Mr. Nice is followed by the 3 very large black men and doesn't even Care what's in the metal box from the ship anymore. He drives the Ford carefully through traffic, one black man is sitting beside him and one is in the back seat. He doesn't have to be told, the men both have those nasty deadly guns. Mr. Nice has locked the metal box in the trunk of one of the cars from the repair shop. When they arrive at the parking lot, he explains ware the box is and the third black man backs his Car up Close to the parked car. Mr. Nice gets out the key and opens the trunk. The box is Covered with a small tarp and still has the cover he placed on it while still on the ship. The first black guy picks up the box with one hand sets it in his Car's trunk. Mr. Nice Can hardly move that box with two hands but this black man does it with one. Mr. Nice steps back and starts to head for the driver's door of the Ford. The second black man holds up a very large paw forcing him to stop. Mr. Nice is waiting expecting to be killed or something worse but isn't. The man hands him an envelope, there is a thick wad of money for him apparently. The three black men get into their car and drive off without a wave or backward glance Mr. Nice doesn't have any idea what is in the metal box from the ship, and is glad, he doesn't like Mr. Big or his band of Mary men.

Mr. Nice just has to stop at a steak place, and decides he has had a rough morning. He orders two steak dinners with a steak, Texas toast, baked potato and pudding for dessert Mr. Nice just loves pudding and eats that first. He doesn't hesitate however and advances to the main Courses. He is getting too fat and tells himself he will start his diet tomorrow this time for sure.

CHAPTER 35

The local Medical Examiner has identified the remains that Barbra's client hooked. The man was a guy from Idaho on vacation to get in a little deep-sea fishing. He was on board a small boat he rented from the marina. Apparently, he got excited while catching a big one and fell in the water. No one knows if the boat drifted away or if he couldn't swim. The Doctor believes that he was taken by sharks just after entering the water. His lungs had some water in them but not completely filled. The sharks have been more active near the location where the victim was found. The authorities want to close that part of the ocean but don't think they can. The area is in the middle of Barbra's favorite fishing spots and will have some effect on her charters. Barbra is waiting at the air strip when Braidy and Carmen finally make it back home. Ben and the other mechanics are surrounding the plane; they say they have missed their plane because it has been gone for so long. Braidy corrects them,

"this is my plane and just take care of her."

Carmen is dressed in a nice skirt and blouse once again and steps down from the plane with grace. She waits until she knows the guys are watching her and bows slightly and says,

"well boys, I thought all this time it was me you were missing, and that I was the prettiest thing around here. Of Course, you must have missed me, but now I'm back, and thank you for the warm welcome.

The guys agree they have missed her and that she is pretty. Braidy sees Barbra waiting for him, she has taken some time to dress in a nice dress and fixed her hair too. She looks very attractive and is standing back from the others. Braidy smiles at her and holds out his hand to her. She walks over to him and takes his hand and folds into his arms. She says,

"Mr. Braidy sir, I have been missing you so, and am oh so glad your back with me."

Braidy tells her that they can go to his house and this time it's his turn to make her dinner Carmen asks,

"may I come too, I mean for the dinner part, you know just for dinner."

Ben tells Carmen that he Can take her over to Headquarters building, he needs to talk with the book keepers about the increased Cost of fuel. The Company buys thousands of gallons of fuel for all the aircraft each month. There are underground tanks that hold lots of various types of fuel and keeping them filled is expensive. Carmen is gracious and doesn't really mind being abandon by Braidy and Barbra, she is glad for them. Ben tells her he will be ready in a minute and goes to the office in the hanger. Carmen says to other guys,

"so, what have you guy's ben wrecking today?"

At first, they are shocked, and then they get it, she is joking with them the way that Jones and Braidy do. They tell her that she had better buy lots of insurance, that is if she wants to Continue flying with that Braidy fellow. He is turning Jamaican it looks like. Carmen smiles big and says,

"what a lucky guy, to get a girl as pretty as Barbra that is. At least he gets a girl to look at him, you old dogs Can't even get a girl to talk to you."

Well what about you, you're talking to us?" Carmen shakes her delicate head Causing her Curls to bounce,

"well, you see boys, Rose pays me to talk to you guys, to ensure that the planes can still fly."

Mac looks at his boys and says,

"I'm not sure, but I think we've been insulted."

Ben Comes out with papers in a brief Case and invites Carmen to ride with him in a new blue over blue four-wheel drive pickup. The truck is new and smells like it. Carmen finds the door and after opening it wonders how she will ever get her foot high enough to get in this beast without exposing her secret places. Ben sees her dilemma and brings a bucket for her. He places the bucket upside down by the open door and Carmen thanks him and steps right up in.

CHAPTER 36

Mr. Big has a plan, he always has a plan. The plan isn't really anything brilliant, it is clever. Mr. Big will use Mr. Nice to apply as Captain on one of Roses container ships. Mr. Big doesn't think much of Mr. Nice, after all he is a big fat slob. Mr. Big has provided Mr. Nice with orders and enough money that he Can purchase the materials needed. Mr. Nice doesn't read his new orders until he gets a good night's rest and has had time to Calm down. Mr. Nice needs time to recover from visits to Mr. Biggs because of the hired help mostly. Although he doesn't like Mr. Big either. He wishes things Could be simple again, it uses to be that all he had to do was kill off a few people and Call it good. Mr. Nice has to be so stern acting as a ship's Captain Mr. Nice reads over the orders and sighs; he needs to find another line of work. Being a ship's Captain isn't easy for him to play. He will have to read up on regulations and all that other Crap. Those Container ships are so big; some are more than 1300 feet long and Carry thousands of Containers. He doesn't know what else he will have to do as Captain on one of Roses ships. The ship is called the Kenneth something or other, apparently named after Roses father

The ship will dock in San Diego, just a few days now. Mr. Nice will have to study hard for a while to learn enough to BS his way through. Mr. Nice will have to gets some fake documents and create some sort of records of past work. What a pain in the royal but, he is basically a peaceful man, just wanting to be left alone. He has to stop with the fast food and that will really hurt. Mr. Nice does enjoy his fast food and actually any food

Mr. Nice does manage to stop eating junk food and forces down salads and vegetables. He walks more and finds a gym and works out. The sweat pores off him smelling like fries and burgers and who knows what. He Can look pretty good if he tries. After two weeks, he is another man, he admires himself in his new uniform trousers and shirt too. He will get new Clothes after being hired by Roses people. He has documents that are Convincing, and even he believes them. He changes his voice by talking lower and deeper in his Chest. He develops a faraway look in his eye like he just knows. He Can play any part with a little practice and declares himself ready for an interview. Mr. Nice travels to Seattle to the headquarters building and up to the main office. When he arrives, there are five people waiting for him. The man who greets him first is none other than Jones. Mr. Nice has to swallow at first sight of Jones. He is relieved soon after, Jones doesn't recognize him at all. At a stone table are the rest. There is a young and very pretty Spanish girl, and after looking twice he sees that she is blind. He thinks that this will be easier than he thought.

The second woman is Rose herself, also quite beautiful. And one more woman a black woman, who looks troubled. She is probably pretty too, but her face is unsmiling. The other guy is a tall man, Mr. Nice remembers the name, Braidy.

The blind woman who introduces herself as Carmen, invites him to please sit with them. She asks if he would like some Coffee or anything else to drink? Mr. Nice is impressed with this lovely young woman, she is Cool. He sits a short distance from the others at the end. He Can see them all without turning his head much. All at once Coming from another part of the large room is a huge dog. The dog must weigh at least 200 pounds. The dog doesn't look fat, he is just really big. The dog Comes Close to Mr. Big but not Close enough to bite he hopes. The dog goes over to Jones and settles down beside him.

Rose starts,

"Mr. Martin, we'd like to welcome you to our Company, your Credentials are impressive and all your documentation is in order too." "are there any questions you have for any of us?"

Just for a moment Mr. Nice now Captain Martin wishes that he was a real ship's Captain working for this very nice woman. She is gracious and thoughtful, she looks him right in the eye and leaves no doubt as to her meaning of her words. Mr. Nice now Captain Martin has practiced his very white smile and flashes her his pearly whites. He has worked on his teeth and even gone to a dentist for polishing and whitening. He study's his smile in the mirror and knows he looks good. He stays Cool and says,

"no mam, everything looks good to me, and I am looking forward to serving as Captain on your ship. I will need some input from time to time if you don't mind, I'm sure you have Certain ways you like things done? Rose smiles back, she is very beautiful, and tells him, that's fine, they will let him know. She tells him he Can always Call in to the office. She Continues, we provide all of our Captains with satellite phones we all use. We have found the phones Can Call anywhere and Can be Called most anywhere. Most routes you will be plying are on the main routes and there shouldn't be any Communication problem for you. Rose goes on, asking if the salary is acceptable? Captain Martin forgot to look at that, he doesn't miss a beat and tells her its fine, thank you. He doesn't care what the salary may be, Mr. Big will grab it anyway, Captain Martin will be offered a few Coins from one of Mr. Biggs thugs.

Mr. Nice notices that the big black dog keeps looking at him like he might be lunch. That dog knows something is up, and he thinks it's a good thing the mutt Can't talk. Captain is provided company uniforms in his size, and he has to admit that the blue Colors are Cheery and refreshing

Captain Martin is driven off to the airport, by Joe. He will fly to San Diego where he will move over to his new ship. The ship looks bigger every time he sees it. Of course, a ship doesn't get bigger, it just looks that way. The new Captain just tries to look invisible when crossing the gang plank and walking across that big huge deck. He finds the elevator and pushes a button labeled bridge. He puts on his stern face and thinks lemon. He arrives on the bridge, and finds theirs no one there. Where is the Crew, he looks around? Captain remembers that this ship is automated, and wonders if he should just call out. He decides to give it a try,

"say ship, where is everyone?"

There is a screen with letters appearing locating the ship's crew. Captain Martin likes that, he Can know where everyone is while standing on the bridge.

Captain Martin looks around the bridge, its fully automated, but still someone has to do a few things. He reflects on the name he chose, Captain Martin, he was surprised that no one mentioned that his last name Martin is the same as Roses last name. Oh well, he guesses it really doesn't matter.

CHAPTER 37

Barbra has replaced the engine in her cabin cruiser, she hired boat mechanics to do the job. She and Braidy have moved in together, and live in one house or the other. They just get up earlier if they need to travel further. Joni has decided to move into one of the apartments in the headquarters building. Rose doesn't charge any rent for Joni or Carmen. She is impressed with Joni; she keeps many angry clients away from Rose or Carmen. Joni felt a little disappointment when she heard that Braidy and that island girl are living together. She supposes that it's her own fault, she could have done more to catch that Braidy fellow. Joni enjoys her work, and the girls get together with baby Nance for some woman talk. Joni has gotten computers with voice over capabilities and a smart phone. Carmen has been a big help and she and Joni compare information and knowledge.

Nancy is calmer mostly, she was worried about Melvin's body showing up but no, theirs nothing. Barbra tells Nancy that she has never seen anything survive that spot where Mr. Melvin got himself to. Nancy believes her, after all she definitely knows about the ocean. Barbra is a very interesting woman. She has many clients again, people forget old news. Barbra thinks she should paint her house, it is gray now but she thinks it would look better in yellow. She likes yellow, it's so cheery, or who knows why. She just likes yellow and will paint the house. Barbra looks at her house all the way around. The house is large and will take about 20 gallons or more. She walks Closer to a wall and scrapes the boards with her fingernails. The paint flakes a little but not bad.

Barbra mentions the house painting project to Braidy and he tells her he will help, and he can paint her house using the paint sprayer the company paints equipment with, and will work on a house too. Braidy comes with Barbra after he has finished with work for the day. She has fixed herself up some, she looks Charming. She has a grill behind the house and has a Couple of nice thick steaks. She uses her best Cooking skills to grill the steaks, she made potato salad and has fresh vegetables for a toss salad.

    Braidy and Barbra walk around the grounds while the steaks are Cooking, she has the fire banked and the meat will take a while to finish. The grounds around Barbra's house are wild, everything needs trimming and she has been doing some but not enough. At one time, someone was quite a gardener, and she Can see the former flower beds. There are flowering trees and fruit trees too. Barbra works at it when she has time and Braidy says it looks good. He doesn't know one flower from another but likes the colors. Barbra has visited Roses roof top greenhouse and just loves her different kinds of roses. The smell is so sweet inside the greenhouse that Barbra Could stay there all day. Rose has a water feature that bubbles softly. There is lawn Chairs close to the water and anyone can visit for a little peace and quiet. Rose wishes she had made the greenhouse bigger, but doesn't change anything.

CHAPTER 38

Captain Martin alias Mr. Nice gets settled into the Captain's Cabin on board the container ship. The crew are indifferent and go about doing their jobs. He issues orders that he thinks are appropriate and the men carry them out, but there's no Camaraderie.

Mr. Big pats himself on the back, he thinks he has a perfect solution for moving illegal product. The boxes that Captain Martin brings aboard the ships are heavy. The boxes are lined with led for the weight, and inside the led box is high grade heroin powder. Mr. Big believes that the led will fool everyone into thinking that something besides heroin is inside the boxes. Captain doesn't even know what's in the boxes, he just moves them onto the ships as personal luggage. He uses a luggage Cart to move the heavy box, along with other personal luggage. The Captain likes to stay a shore whenever the ship gets to a port. He has to meet someone he doesn't know and will never see again for the delivery. He doesn't know how the delivery guy knows where to meet him, what hotel he will stay at, but someone is always there.

So far, the new system is working just fine, ships Captains have a lot of freedoms in foreign ports. Captain Martin has the respect of local authorities probably because of the uniform he wares. Once he comes a shore he zips through the business in good time. No one on the ship wants to hang around with him, it's really true that the Captain is all alone on a ship. Captain Martin is tempted all the time to find good things to eat. He needs to be careful of his weight. He is one of those guys that only has to look at food and gain pounds. The boxes are taken out of ships in the U.S. along with his other luggage, no one seems to care. Captain Martin is instructed to meet with Mr. Big, and the masquerade begins anew. The same big bad black guys are waiting for him when he gets away from the dock area. He is taken by surprise, no one told him of any meeting. They snicker at his uniform, he isn't so important with these three. He is pushed into a van this time; the vehicle has no windows in the back and people Can't see what's in the back. Captain is driven to a Motel on the edge of

town, it's a flee trap. The bad boys aren't gentle with him and he falls on a knee tearing his trousers. They laugh at him and drag him up by one arm. Mr. Big isn't in sight when he enters the room. Shortly he Comes out of the bathroom, with yet another mask. Today's disguise is a Superman mask. He has that little box in his hand that disguises his voice too. Mr. Big Chooses to stand for this visit and Captain Martin is forced to sit on the edge of the bed. Mr. Big,

"you did alright this time, that is for a dummy."

Captain is shivering in his shoes, he isn't suckered in by a Comment like that. Mr. Big stares at him and shakes his head in disappointment. Captain Martin has no idea what the problem is, he just waits. Mr. Big hands him his new orders himself this time. The orders are in a business envelope and it looks really fat. He waits until Mr. Big gives him the go away wave and he leaves slowly. When he gets outside, the three bad guys aren't there, instead theirs a taxi Cab waiting. The Cabby asks him,

"where too Mr.?"

Captain Martin decides to go back to the ship, he has a bottle or two of whisky for medicinal purposes only of course.

The ship is being unloaded with cranes working from every position, they hook onto a Container and lift the boxes up and off the ship. Some of the boxes go onto special trailers behind semi tractors and in an instant, are fastened down and off they go. There is a regular assembly line of trucks ready to carry away the containers. additional containers are stacked on shore waiting for other transportation methods. Each container holds tons of cargo from toy trains to clothing to auto parts. Everything is shipped by container including humans some times. Not this trip, well at least Captain Martin doesn't think so, he cannot tell what's in those containers, theirs only numbers. Captain Martin takes the elevator to his cabin and finds someone waiting for him by the door. The man is tall, about 6 foot 2 and has gray hair. He is dress well in a gray suit, the man looks to be in good shape. The man introduces himself as Jim Smith. Captain Martin knows a phony when he sees one, and this guy is no exception. He has government written all over him He probably is armed and is wearing a bullet proof vest too. The gray-haired man, Jim Smith tells Captain Martin he has a few questions. Captain can't help but swallow before answering,

"how can I help Mr. Smith?"

Smith motions towards the Cabin door and looks at Martin. He gets it and invites Smith in. The cabin boy has been by lately and the room looks clean and neat. There are comfortable chairs in a half circle and they each take a chair. Mr. Smith begins,

"Captain Martin, you're not in trouble, we have a few questions, the questions are about your boss, Rose is her name I believe. Mr. Nice is so relieved that the questions aren't about him he actually sighs. Smith thinks he is frustrated or board. Smith,

"I understand that this Rose person inherited the company from her Father? The company is still shipping and moving containers?"

Captain tells him, that Roses company hasn't been shipping containers all that long, these ships are relatively new. The red and white ships are the older ones, but there aren't many of those left. Rose is wanting to ship more containers, and there are fifty of the latest models in service now.

Smith wants to know about other employees working for Rose, and Captain can truthfully tell him he doesn't know. Smith brings out a stack of documents laying them on a coffee table. The papers are filled with numbers, and Captain has no idea what they mean. Smith says these numbers indicate profit and losses from the past 10 years. He says to Captain that the company was losing money when Ken was managing and after Rose took over it began to show a profit. The government wants to know why, and does he know of any illegal activity's? Martin again Can tell the truth, no nothing, he knows not a thing. The G. man brings up a drawing of a man's face.

Captain Martin, Mr. Nice, nearly falls on the floor with one look. He sees himself in another disguise, off to the side. He sees the three thugs loading Jones and Braidy from Roses container ship. But also, unknown to him, he was captured by a Camera too. He is wearing one of his masks, and their he is. Whoever drew the picture is really good, and even the edges of the mask are visible

Mr. Smith understands that this man doesn't know anything about Roses Company. Ever since the Chinese women were discovered on Roses Container ship . The Feds have been watching. So far, they have discovered nothing. They have been observing Captain Martin and wonder at all the luggage he takes ashore. They have no reason to suspect him however and continue to watch him.

Jim Smith, comes to the headquarters building and requests a visit with Jones. Jones has his own office on a lower floor. When Smith arrives in the outer office Jones's secretary is nice enough but somewhat chilly. Jones has windows overlooking the harbor, and the view is interesting. Jones has his office on the 15th floor and the view isn't bad. Jones recognizes Mr. Smith as a government type and looks unhappy. Smith asks,

"Mr. Jones, I have a few questions concerning this company before Ken died. The question is about profit and loss. There are certain discrepancies we need to know more about."

Jones tells him that he knows nothing about the company's finances before he came to work here. The problem seems to be that no one knows anything about these money differences. Although there's not a huge amount, the amounts are steady. For 11 years, Big Lift Salvage and Shipping lost money. The company retained enough assets and cash flow to be able to stay in business. Jones doesn't like this guy or any government types and wouldn't answer any of Smith's questions even if he knew the answers.

Mr. Smith is getting nowhere with this smart-ass Jones and packs up and leaves in a huff. Jones knows the creep will go after Rose eventually and calls her,

"Rose here, what can I do for you?"

Jones doesn't give his usual answer, instead sounds serious,

"I think there's a fed coming up there to ask about some past financial records, probably from when Ken ran the business.'"

Rose asks him if he will come up too? Jones tells her that he's on his way and steps out his office. He can't help thinking, what a difference in his life from a dairy farmer to whatever he is now. Jones uses the private elevator and gets to the top floor long before Mr. Smith using the public elevator. Rose and Carmen share the big office, they each have their own desk in different spaces of the room. The model rail road has been removed and the fish tanks are gone too. Rose has had a new carpet installed; it is of Course blue over blue. Jones looks for Jack and is told that he is walking around the building with Nancy. Jones calls her on the communicators they all use. She is in the basement garage and says she will be right up. She will use the private elevator and arrives with Jack shortly. Jones and Rose decide to be polite but reserved, anything they might say could be used against them later. Rose doesn't know much more than Jones accept she knows more details. She knows that Ken was stealing from his own company but not exactly why. The company is well established and has been doing business for many years. At one time Ken or his Father must have been honest enough to build peoples trust. There is a new girl at the outer receptionist desk and she calls on Carmen's intercom. She tells Carmen that a Mr. Jim Smith would like to talk with her. Carmen decides to try and deal with this character herself, she goes over to the office door opens it and invites Mr. Smith in. There is an arrangement of Comfortable chairs Close to the door that they use for visitors they want to keep distant. Mr. Smith offers her his hand; she shakes it loosely and invites him to please sit down. She asks him if he wants some Coffee or something else. Mr. Smith is impressed with this young lady's manners and understands why Roses company is so successful. Carmen takes a chair around the curve from Smith, and asks,

"so, Mr. Smith, how can I help please?"

Smith wants to know about some old financial records he has before him in a large stack of print outs. He talks fast, thinking that he will overwhelm this young lady but hasn't got a chance. Carmen is experienced at listening to details and holds up her small hand,

"Mr. Smith stop right their sir, I didn't work for this company back then, I am relatively new."

Mr. Smith tells her that he really wants to talk to Rose. Carmen decides to give this G man a bad time. She says that he will need to make an appointment before visiting the boss lady. He isn't happy about that and she Can hear him grumbling. She gets out her note taker device to make an appointment for him. For the first-time Smith notices that she is blind, and doesn't know what to say. She knows what's going on, she has used her blindness to her own advantage. She is polite and efficient, she tells him that Rose has some time in two weeks. Mr. Smith knows he is being put on by this youngster. He says that he may get a Court order before his next visit. Just than Jack comes ambling over to Carmen, she lays her small hand on his big head. Jack and Carmen understand one another and Jack gives Mr. Jim Smith the evil eye. Mr. Smith works out often and isn't any kind of weakling but even he shivers when Jack stairs at him with those very intense brown eyes. Jack opens his mouth in a yawn revealing a very fine Collection of very large teeth. Mr. Smith decides to beat a hasty retreat and gets up to go. Jack has to have a little fun with this guy and blocks his retreat. Mr. Smith in a higher voice asks,

"excuse me mam, Could you call off your dog?"

Carmen,

"oh, he's not my dog, he just hangs around here looking for something to munch on, and well sometimes, before we Can stop him, he has government types for lunch."

By this time, Mr. Smith is thinking about pulling his gun when Nancy Comes strolling over, and she is looking good. She has a Combat harness with a fully loaded belt. She wears a uniform that is well fitted and follows her Curves for sure, but also outlines her strengths. Nancy,

"Oh Come on now Jack, you already had two of these guys from the government for breakfast."

Jack looks at Nancy and back at Smith than licks his nose with his enormous tongue. Mr. Smith steps around the dog staying Close to Nancy and heads for the door. Just than good old Mr. Braidy Comes singing in to the office. Without anyone noticing he landed on the roof top and is of course hungry again. He is taller than Mr. Smith and is friendly. Jack knows a good thing when he sees it or rather smells it and proceeds to the kitchen. Rose has been preparing lunch for Braidy, she enjoys feeding her favorite Uncle as she calls him. Mr. Smith tries to leave with some sort of dignity but blows it. He has to swallow before another try. By that time, the door is hitting him on his very special but, he has changed his mind about trying to be tough. Jones has been watching and listening to Carmen and Jacks performances and smiles to himself. The entire event has been recorded by hidden Cameras and like all visits Mr. Smith was covered as well. Mr. Smith is escorted by several of Nancy's security folks and Mr. Smith thinks he is glad to get out of the building in one peace. The problem for Mr. Smith is that government mucky mucks don't exactly approve of what he is doing. There isn't enough evidence to obtain a subpoena, or a search warrant it's all Circumstantial. The last person that Mr. Smith hears is Joni,

"have a good day Mr. Smith, thanks for dropping in."

Smith wonders how did that woman get his name so quickly, he never saw her on the way in. He says to himself,

"I think I need a drink."

CHAPTER 39

Mr. Big is wondering how long that dummy, Nice; will keep following orders. He might develop a backbone and actually stand up for himself. The metal inside the box isn't led at all, its gold. The gold is painted to look like led although he doubts that good old Mr. Nice has ever opened the boxes. He has to admit that Nice Can really play a part, he Can be anyone. Mr. Big wonders if Mr. Nice Could imitate Jones, although Jones is taller, still elevator shoes Could raise Nice up enough. Mr. Big has kept three Chinese girls for his personal use. He has introduced them to the magic white powder and they are truly hooked. They do anything he tells them, and they eat like birds, a little rice, some beans, and their good Mr. Big has a house boat and moves it often, the phones and other services he doesn't need, every utility he needs is on board. The house boat is 120 feet long with a huge bedroom, and of course a King-sized bed. He and the three girls can all sleep comfortably on the bed. The bath is huge also, like a small swimming pool. The things those girls do for him in the shower and on the bed, is really fun. Mr. Big moves the boat himself; he takes it slow, not such a good boat driver. One of the girls has gotten herself pregnant somehow, and will be out of action for a week or two. The other two do alright and serve him well. Mr. Big knows he gets too fat if he doesn't work it off and so he works out. He has an exercise room on his boat and he goes there once a day. The girls never need to lose weight, if anything they are too thin. One girl is almost 12 years old and is developing nicely. He has to Chuckle at that one, nicely for Mr. Nice. If Nice only knew what happens on board this boat, he would sing a different tune.

Mr. Nice, isn't the swinger like Mr. Big but he has a Chinese girl who actually likes him. She Comes from a family that has some money. She doesn't let Nice just push her around, she knows what she wants and can get it. She spends time with him whenever he is in her home town. She comes on the ship for a visit and admires the ship. The ship is impressive especially the accommodation block. The cabins are plush with deep Carpeting and gold fixtures in the bathrooms. The ship Cook is excellent with a variety of dishes that suits anyone's pallet. Captain Martin tries to advance his knowledge of this pretty Chinese girl but she shuts him down. He wants to know her better and offers her bribes such as delicious dishes from the galley, fine wines, and even jewelry but no, no, no. Captain doesn't give up; he knows that sooner or later he will have his way. The other crew members are at least standing at attention when he arrives on the bridge, and he acknowledges them. The crew are from everywhere and speak five different languages, thankfully the all speak English.

The young Chinese girl isn't stupid; she knows she will get this rich American Captain in time. She dresses to kill and tempts him at every opportunity. She stays just out of reach but near enough that he Can get a whiff of her very expensive perfume. She wears clothes that are light and revealing. She notices the other crew members are watching her too, and she gives them a tiny bit of attention.

Captain invites her to sail with them when they depart in the morning and she thinks about that. If she does go with him, she will have to sleep with him which means her greatest asset will be revealed. She likes the thought but isn't sure that's the right thing for her to do. Finally, she decides she will go once, she has never sailed on the open ocean before. She marvels at this huge ship with its blue over darker blue Colors. The blues are so rich that she gets lost in their depths. Someone Chooses wisely when deciding on them for this ship. The Captain's uniform is the same blue like the Crew too. The ship is like magic, the Crew just talk to the ship and it obeys. She Could drive a ship like this one, or do you Call making a ship go something else.

Captain gets the usual message and collects the shipment. The box seems lighter this time and he wonders if he is getting stronger.

He shrugs it off and piles luggage on his two-wheeled luggage cart. Everything from the dock onto the ship is easy, no steps to grunt heavy baggage up. He Can roll right along from the dock onto the ship.

CHAPTER 40

Braidy and Carmen are flying out to another lumber camp on one of the King Airs. The planes are close enough in age that they are virtually identical. Jones says he can tell a difference in flying but Braidy can't. Maybe Jones has differing abilities who can say. Jones is talking to new people who are interested in working on the container ships. They need everyone from Captains right on down to cabin boys. They aren't Called cabin boys any more, they have proper titles of course but Jones is old fashioned. Braidy and Carmen will fly to the Carolina's and check up on the new powerlines and the new saw in Georgia too. Carmen has found electric wire and enough poles to Complete the new service. The project cost a great deal, and she shudders at the expenses. Rose doesn't worry about it; she has done this kind of thing many times before. She tells Carmen that she is doing a good job and just keep it up. Carmen has two smart phones now and two lap tops computers. The computers are as big as she Can get in a lap top model and when she is carrying both she looks like she is moving into a new house. She is strong for her size and doesn't complain however she is secretly relieved when Braidy simply reaches out and takes them both for her. She really likes Mr. Braidy especially since he and that Barbra have been hanging out together. He was nice before but is even nicer now he has a woman. Carmen wonders what that would be like to have a man to be with every night. Braidy goes through the Check list and starts the engines, and when they line up asks,

"are we ready?"

Carmen tells him yes,

"do I have a choice?"

Braidy shoves the throttles forward and they are roaring down the runway and lift into a partly Cloudy sky.

They land at Atlanta International Airport and rent a medium sized Car for the trip to the camp. The camp is busy, there are three utility trucks drilling holes for the new poles and two more smaller trucks stringing the new wire. The poles look very black because of the Creosote. The poles smell strong and Can be noticed form a mile away. The power Company people are keeping their part of the bargain. They have a dozer Clearing the route pushing down trees and leveling the parts of the route that the pole trucks Cannot get through. The trucks have a tower that raises up when in use with a 12-inch drill bit on the end. Behind the trucks are trailers full of poles, when the hole is drilled, the operator lifts the next pole swings it around and slides it into the hole. The equipment Can hold the pole straight up and tamp the dirt in around the pole. The new poles look nice and neat all aligned in a row. The project will be finished in a week according to the boss. Carmen and Braidy are standing nearby watching and listening to Carson explaining the procedure. Carmen isn't interested at all in what's being said. She wants to examine one of those hole-digging trucks for herself. She is waring genes and a sweat shirt so being a girl isn't a problem. She has to always remember where she is going and dress accordingly. She always wares genes and a sweat shirt to the woods.

Carmen is standing next to Braidy and she asks him if he will tell her what one of those pole trucks looks like. Braidy doesn't mind at all, he tells her that the trucks have 8 wheels in the back with a flat bed. On the flat bed is a boom that raises up straight in the air. The boom has a Cable winch that lifts the pole up, and also theirs a shaft with the drill bit on the bottom end. The truck drives along the line stopping, drilling a hole than placing the pole in the hole than packing the dirt around the pole. The entire process takes less than five minutes per pole. The poles are already equipped with insulators for the wire to be Connected to. Carmen is interested in anything mechanical, after all she needs to know about equipment to be able to talk intelligently. She thanks Braidy and says,

"should we be doing something now?"

Braidy asks,

"like what, lunch maybe?"

She tugs on his arm and tells him he is silly. Braidy smiles and admits that he probably is, is that alright? Braidy looks around at other things at the camp sight. He tells Carmen that the new saw is set up, and it looks massive. She wants to really get a good touch of that one. After all its her job to know these things. She will examine the saw after lunch or she likes to say, Brady's noon fueling stop

The camp workers are out cutting timber trimming off limbs and bringing the logs to the new mill. That way they will have a good supply of logs to start with when the sawmill is up and running. They use bright yellow dozers with Cable wrenches and blades on the front. They work together as a team, pointing an waving at each other since the Diesel engines are so loud. The chainsaws are loud too and the men wear ear protectors.

When it's almost noon all the guys troop over to the log building for some hardy lunch. The Cook is a grandmotherly black lady who loves everyone and wants to feed the world. She looks like she enjoys her own cooking being almost as round as she is tall. The men just think she is wonderful and Call her Mom. She isn't any of their Moms of Course but she doesn't mind at all. This day is beef stew cooked in a giant pot, and as the cooking continues more and more go into the pot. She puts so many different vegetables in there that she couldn't tell you the recipe even if she wanted to. She has a name but everyone Calls her Cookie Mom of course. She has baked Corn bread, and prepared salad makings and pies.

Carson invites the workers from the power pole project as well and the dinner hall is crowded. Carmen decides to stay out of the line of fire, after all she is tiny and might get squashed in the mad rush to the trough. She finds a small table in the kitchen and pores herself a Cup of tasty coffee. She didn't use to like coffee but has been influenced by all the others. She is noticed by Cookie Mom and she asks,

"Why honey, you don't have to be out here all by you self."

Carmen smiles big as she can and says,

"oh, that's alright mam, I need a little quiet sometimes."

Cookie Mom,

"why you pore child you're blind, I'm so sorry, what Can I get you?"

Carmen has been down this road before and handles it well. She tells Cookie Mom that it's nothing, she does just fine without it. Carmen knows that the best thing to do is to get the conversation going toward the other woman. People always want to talk about themselves.

After lunch, the men go back to work and the roaring of Diesels and chain saws fill the air. The hole digging trucks are nearly finished, and the wire stringers are Closing in. The transformer has already been placed near the saw mill and only needs to be Connected. The work goes on all afternoon and Carmen grows sleepy. She wants to find a place to take a nap but knows she had better not. She asks Braidy if he is sleepy? Braidy is more than sleepy, he is sound asleep. Other workers are putting down their equipment and are rubbing their eyes and yawning. Carmen is hearing alarms going off in her head but cannot do anything about them. The crew digging holes for the poles have moved their truck and the digger is going into the ground. The hole is complete and the boom swings around for a pole. The operator is slow reacting and the pole isn't stopped before smashing into several camp men standing near for an afternoon smoke. The pole is 30 feet long and many men are struck. The pole is sideways and hits all of them. The pole stops after Completing its ark. The men Call out in pain, that is those who are still alive. The operator stairs in horror at what he has done. He manages to shut everything down and grabs his Chest. The accident has stopped everything and the only ones who are still Conscious are Cookie Mom and Carmen. Carmen wasn't hungry at lunch and didn't eat much. Cookie Mom did the Cooking. Carmen tries to wake Braidy but he is down for the count. She is blind and terrified and wishes she had a gun. Carmen isn't afraid of much but this accident if that is what it is, scares her. Carmen hears Cookie Mom Calling her and wonders what she can do, she isn't a large woman weighing 110 pounds. She is having trouble thinking, her head is fuzzy. Not so fuzzy though to not recognize she is in danger. She believes that if she is still awake and Cookie Mom is still awake than maybe Cookie Mom may be the guilty party.

Carmen is on the ground beside Braidy, she can feel him breathing under her hand. His heart is thumping away just as it should. She decides to play dumb and falls over Brady's chest. She isn't heavy, but still tries to hold most of her weight off of his chest. She wants to be near him so she can feel him breathing. She is thinking as hard as she can, Braidy please wake up. Braidy must have heard her, and groans. She is so surprised at that she forgets to act asleep. Braidy has a fast metabolism and goes through foods faster than other folks. Thanks to his energy Consumption he is Coming around. She tells him to lay still, play dead. Braidy likes her laying on his Chest and says ok. She smiles at him, thinking,

"you dirty old man, you wonderful dirty old man you."

Braidy gets the picture and looks around with nearly Closed eyes. He tells her that Cookie Mom has gone back into the building. Carmen says,

"what do we do?"

Braidy tells her to stay cool, let's see what happens, that cook person may not be alone. Carmen hasn't thought of that, and says so.

Braidy is thinking and tells Carmen that they should run to the rental Car and get some help. This doesn't feel right, we don't know what that old lady is up to. Carmen is trying to remember where the rental car is,

"where is the rental car she asks?"

Braidy is trying to look around while still appearing to be asleep. He finally sees it, it's a Couple of hundred yards away. He sees a man with a gas can splashing gasoline inside the Car and on the outside. Just as he is about to tell Carmen the nasty news a big whoomph and the pretty red Car is quickly turning black. Carmen asks,

"that sounds like a bon-fire to me."

Braidy tells her that their rental Car is burning, and theirs a guy over there who started the fire. Carmen wants to Climb inside Braidy for protection. Braidy decides to dash for the machine shed, its metal and won't burn. He is afraid the bad guys will burn down the entire Camp. He tells Carmen what he has in mind, and she says,

"do you think there's a truck in there we Can use?"

Braidy tells her he doesn't see any trucks through the door way but there is a D8 Cat sitting there bright yellow and looking pretty. Carmen doesn't feel like laughing at that, she is really scared. Braidy looks around and sees the fire bug Coming toward them. They have not moved but still he looks like he knows something. Braidy is feeling stronger and Carmen was not affected that much in the first place. They jump up and run for the machine shed. The guy Coming toward them is surprised and shouts out for them to stop. Carmen is really moving, Braidy Can hardly keep up with her. Her shorter legs must be moving really fast, he is taking giant steps but she is pulling on his hand. Carmen is a tough gal and Braidy is encouraged with her energy. They arrive at the shed without being killed by gunfire and Braidy looks around. Carmen notices the machine smells, oil, grease, Diesel fuel and that new paint smell from the dozer. Braidy tells Carmen that there's no trucks, mostly broken junk. He asks,

"I don't suppose you know how to drive a dozer do you?"

Carmen tells him it doesn't matter; she will drive the dam thing anyhow. Braidy leads her over to the Cat and she Climbs up the steps. There is a full cab, with a door that Can close. The Cat is just being stored there until it may be needed. Braidy tells her that the key is in the ignition and he can figure it all out. Carmen slides over from the Dorr to make room for Braidy. He sees the bad guy Coming with a friend or two. When he tells Carmen that, she says to shut the door and lock it if he Can. Braidy shuts the door but there's no lock. He turns the key and just like that it starts up. They have really made starting Diesels easier since he was a kid. His father was in the Construction business and had many types of heavy equipment. The ones he remembered had pony motors, little engines to start the big ones. The two bad guys coming, are joined by two more and just stand there. Braidy wonders how bullet resistant the glass in the windshield might be. He pulls back a lever and the 10-foot blade Come up providing some protection. The blade is heavy duty and will stop any bullet. Carmen wants to know what's going on? Braidy tells her that there are 4 guys now. He says that they have guns of course. Carmen asks,

"do you have your gun with you?"

Braidy admits he left it in the glove box in the rental car. Carmen knows he feels stupid for that and says,

"Oh that's ok, you probably Couldn't hit the broad side of a barn with the dam thing even if you were trying."

Braidy has to think about that one, he isn't sure what she means. Actually, she doesn't either and tells him she's sorry. Braidy knows she is scared like him and says things just to be talking. Braidy can get down low in the cab and Carmen Can squeeze behind the seat. Braidy looks behind him and sees Cookie Mom holding a shot-gun. That old lady doesn't look like her former self. She looks much thinner and much whiter. Braidy recognizes her because of the apron she is waring. He tells Carmen of the new danger, and asks her what does she want to do. Carmen says,

"you're the big tough guy, you're supposed to protect little old me from these dangers."

Braidy, admits that he blew it by leaving his gun in the car. She tells him it's alright, she doesn't have one either. Braidy knows that dozers don't move very fast, they are built for power not speed. He selects the faster gear and gets ready to pop the Clutch. He shoves open the throttle and a Cloud of black smoke puffs out of the smoke stack. The dozer vibrates with power and when he lets out the Clutch the huge yellow machine Creeps forward. They won't win any races with this turtle. Braidy doesn't worry, he points his new weapon at the middle of the bad guys. They lift up their guns and bang away at the steel blade in front. Sparks fly off the metal making winning sounds. The gun shots are small caliber and don't do much damage to the dozer. The shot gun from behind shatters the rear window getting glass over them both. Carmen lets out a little scream hardly noticeable with the roaring Diesel. Braidy pushes on the throttle lever but that's all she wrote; they are traveling at a lightning fast 4 miles per hour. Braidy glances back at Cookie Mom or whatever she is now and sees that she is pointing the gun at them again. He tells Carmen to scrunch down lower and she gives out a small noise that might have been ok.

Braidy just keeps on moving forward, the bad guys have no effect on stopping the yellow giant. The Diesel is roaring and Braidy in his excitement has bumped a knob that turns on the radio. The radio plays Johnny Cash grumbling out, Walk The line. The extra noise is louder than the Diesel and the bad guys look at each other wondering,

"what the hell!"

The four bad guys aren't worried, they know that dozer Can't go fast and so anything the this Crazy Braidy does won't matter. Braidy rolls through the doors and over the dirt, he hasn't any idea what to do or where to go. Carmen is wanting to know what's going on please. He forgot her for just a moment and tells her they have moved out of the machine shed. The bad guys just shrug and step aside. The bad woman Comes over to the other four and they seem to be watching in amusement.

CHAPTER 41

Braidy heads for one of the trucks, he Can drive them out of here. When they arrive at the nearest truck, he parks the dozer beside the driver's door of the truck. He helps pore Carmen out of the Cab and into the truck. He tells her to get down on the floor and keep her pretty head down. She doesn't hesitate and rolls herself into a little ball. Braidy looks back at the boom noticing that is still attached to the pole that smashed so many men. Braidy has never run a boom like that and has no idea how. He finds that the trucks engine is still running, and selects a gear than lets out the Clutch. The bad guys just stand there not moving, and he says to Carmen,

"Why do you suppose they're not trying to stop us?"

Carmen has an idea and says,

"I am afraid it's because we're white."

Braidy groans,

"oh shit, I'll bet your right, these bad guys are here to kill of all the black workers."

Carmen asks,

"isn't that what happened somewhere around here before?"

Braidy allows that it did, he and Jones witnessed what happened and some old cook Came blasting through the bad guys using a CJ5 as a bowling ball. Those guys never bothered anyone after that. Carmen wonders if these bad guys could be the same guys? Braidy tells her that he doesn't think it matters, hate is hate; and those who do hate have no limits on what they will do to others. Carmen is asking him if he thinks they can get out of here? Braidy is driving along the edge of the line of new poles. He is watching the boom behind him, not wanting to get it caught on the trees. When they traveled a mile, he stops and tells Carmen he will lock down the boom if he can figure it out. Carmen has studied trucks like this one, and tells him how. Braidy doesn't even wonder any more at Carmen he knows she is always curious with the how's of things and finds out for herself. She is right, the controls are as she says, and the boom swings up and back turning and laying down on its bed. Braidy looks down the trail back towards camp and exclaims,

"they have started the camp on fire, and there's smoke Coming from everywhere. Carmen says,

"those dirty rotten bastards, what kind of assholes are they?"

Braidy is surprised, for some reason he and everyone else believes that Carmen is so innocent

Carmen still has her satellite phone and Calls 911. The dispatcher asks,

"what is your emergency?"

Carmen tells them that the Camp is on fire; all buildings are burning. The dispatcher sounds doubtful and repeats what Carmen has said.

Carmen is getting mad at the stupid idea and forgets her manners.

"listen you reject from the funny farm get you lazy ass moving and come put out these fires please."

The woman is so surprised at the please that she says yes, she will. Braidy is driving as fast as he dares trying not to get Caught on any trees or poles. The trail finally ends at the road that leads to the main road and back to the camp. The truck Climbs onto the gravel and rumbles off toward the small town. Even on a relatively smooth road this truck is no speed daemon and takes forever to get up to 50 miles per hour. Carmen is calling the headquarters building and has to tell Rose some more bad news. Jones answers Roses phone and Carmen is relieved. Jones is sick, remembering what happen the previous year at that camp. Carmen tells Braidy what Jones has told her, he wants to get themselves safe and just wait. He will fly down as fast as he can, and probably Rose will want to come as well. Carmen says to Jones, "we'll be sure and tell that Barbra that her man is just fine, you can also tell her that little oh me protected him from the bad guys, and she needs to take me fishing. Jones says,

"since when are you interested in fishing?"

Carmen tells him that she is interested in everything thank you very much

CHAPTER 42

Captain Martin is high on his new girlfriend she has performed wonderfully well. He is walking around like he is on a cloud. The crew pay no attention to their Captain, who Cares if the bastard got his ashes hauled or not. The girl has a name, although Captain Chooses not to use it, he Calls her Nan. She doesn't mind, it's not a bad name she thinks. Nan comes out of the Captain's cabin late morning waring silk trousers and a loose-fitting blouse, she looks doll like, her hair Comes down her back almost to her ankles She smiles at everyone and the men can't help smiling back. They ask each other,

"now what do you suppose that girl sees in our Captain?"

The ship is traveling at 25 knots and the weather is clear. The ship rides low in the water because of the heavy cargo. The containers are stacked high on the main deck and there are more on the lower decks too. The cargo will be off loaded at Los Angeles and Captain Martin, will no doubt get a request to visit Mr. Big. He remembers his girl Nan and needs to think of something to tell her. She can wait in the Cabin he supposes but probably won't want to stay there. This ship is so wonderful, it practically conns itself. He thinks of himself as just an observer. The crew are efficient however and check the cargo constantly, they are looking for boxes that are Coming loose. The cargo boxes need to be kept tight as possible. If they encounter rough weather, they will be glad the Chains are tight. Shifting Cargo Can cause significant damage even on a ship this large.

The ship arrives in good shape at Los Angeles and the crew are dismissed. Captain is the last to leave the ship. Nan has skipped off the ship as soon as it docks. She said she has some business to do, and will be back in the morning. Captain Martin wonders what that is all about. He sits in his cabin and wonders what to do with himself. There is a knock on the door, and there is one of the black guys that likes to beat him up. The guy isn't rude this time, he just asks for the box. Captain pulls it out from under the bed, noticing its lighter weight. The black guy does too, and looks at Martin. He says,

"hey man, what happen to the gold?"

Martin nearly swallowed his teeth; he knows nothing of any gold. He asks what does the guy mean? The guy says that his box is at least 20 pounds lighter what happen to the blanket blank gold? Captain Martin doesn't have any idea and says that. The black guy is getting mad and stands up. Martin has been thinking about these bad guys, he is tired of being used as a punching bag. Before the bad guy Can pull his own, Captain brings up his shiny new automatic. The man looks with eyes as big as saucers and drops his own gun on the floor. Martin likes that, he had no idea he had that kind of power. Captain decides to get in on the action and demands that the man open the box. The guy doesn't hesitate, and says he will have to get his electric drill from the car. Martin asks,

"where is your car, how far?"

Mr. bad guy tells him that its four blocks from the dock. Martin isn't sure what to do and looks at the box. There are screws holding the box tight together. The screws are different, no drivers like that on this ship. Captain decides to take a Chance, in for penny in for a pound. He tells Mr. bad guy to move out of the Cabin and they ride the elevator to the main deck. When the bad guy steps off the elevator and Captain is standing alone in the doorway three bullets practically take off is head. The other bad guys were waiting amongst the containers. They shot Captain Martin alias Mr. Nice, Captain's uniform isn't a pretty blue any more.

Mr. Big has a passion for small oriental women, and he welcomes Nan to his house boat. The other women are used to new women showing up for those all-night parties. She fits right in; the women are the same size witches very small. Nan has double Crossed Mr. Big and Captain Martin. She has hidden the gold in a place that is so secret that no one else Could find it at least she thinks so. The gold is in five-pound bars and lift right out once the lid is removed.

The paint Comes off easily too, a little scraping with a knife and the gold Comes shining out for all to see. Nan has barrowed only four bars about 20 pounds' worth, figuring this Mr. Pig oops Big won't miss it at all She doesn't know what the exchange rates is these days but 20 pounds is a lot of gold. She doesn't really need any more money; she just likes the thrill of stealing from Mr. Big. Nan is so sweet who could ever suspect her of anything like steeling gold from another crook.

Be leave it or not, Mr. Big has to answer to members higher up on the food chain, he is just as vulnerable as Mr. Nice was.

The three boys are handy, they get Mr. Nice out of the way, they back the Car as Close to the ship as they can. They wrap Captain Bly here up in a blanket from his cabin. There isn't much blood, those direct shots into the head don't bleed much the shooter thought there was, but it's a bottle of catsup the Captain Carries in his shirt pocket under his jacket. Why would anyone carry around a catsup bottle? This Captain fellow was very strange. The catsup looked like blood at first glance but the look is different and the smell isn't blood. The men are all strong and it isn't a problem getting the Captain's dead body into the trunk of the Crown Vick. Since Mr. Nice wasn't using it, they decided to, it's a very Comfortable Car and the truck is made for moving dead people.

CHAPTER 43

In Georgia, the fire department finally arrives at camp but much too late. The fire has gotten out of control and not only the buildings are all gone but the trees are burning too. The fire has gotten to the propane tank behind the dining hall and goes off with a huge fireball that was seen for miles. The camp is a total loss including the new saw mill. The camp workers are all dead those who weren't killed by the power pole were smothered in the fire. The fire department doesn't even try, this fire is too big for them, they just watch like many other gawkers. Carmen and Braidy are waiting for Jones and Rose to fly in, they will meet them at the airport. The King Airs are faster than the earlier models and it won't take as long to fly into the airport. Rose isn't use to these dangers that's for sure, but they have become more familiar. She hugs Carmen than Braidy, glad to find both ok. Carmen knows Rose will get upset hearing details of their escape so she keeps it toned down. Rose doesn't need to know all the details of how she and Braidy almost bought the farm. She thinks that Jones would like that statement; her mind is strange at times like these. Jones and Rose flew over the camp before landing and tells them that the Camp is completely gone. There are trees burning and the fire will probably consume a couple thousand acres. In Georgia, the weather hasn't been as dry as in other places and the damp will slow the fire and finally it runs out, the wood isn't wet but it's far from dry either.

This time there's no hiding bodies by dropping them into the ocean in the dark of night. The fire authorities are already investigating the remains and say they will find out what started the fire. There are 17 people all dead including the guys working on the power lines.

The camp is a total loss including the new mill that hasn't even been paid for yet. What a waste of money, Rose doesn't care as much about the money as the loss of life She is getting tired of these uncalled-for deaths. What in the world makes people do what they do to their fellow man?

The three thugs have gotten rid of Captain Martin, they stuffed him into the trunk of the Crown Vick and will grind up his remains in a wood Chipper, Mr. Nice will simply get blended in with a truck load of ground up trees. The box they will deliver to Mr. Big with an explanation. No doubt Mr. Big will make them go all over the ship to find the 20 pounds of missing gold. Little does Mr. Big know that the answer to the missing gold has been sitting on his lap. Nan is feeling clever, stealing all that gold and placing the blame on that boob of a ship's Captain. She likes her new plan and will make nice with the new Captain too. She never considered herself a thief, rather an opportunist. She despises most men including Mr. Big, she does what she does because she wants it all. Nan has to get back aboard that big ship and remove the missing gold before that ship Can leave port. She doesn't know that Captain Martin is no more, and will be surprised. She used him too, and doesn't care if he is dead. She is truly a greedy woman who looks out for number one.

When Nan can finally get away from the ugly bruit Mr. Big, she hires a cab to take her back to the ship. The ship is being unloaded, no one knows the Captain isn't available. The cranes are moving containers off the ship at a rapid rate and containers are hauled off as soon as they hit the dock. The entire process is organized and Nan has to slip on board between the cranes. She goes to the Captain's Cabin and into a big Closet. The gold is in one of her pieces of tooled leather luggage. She buys only the best for herself and this suitcase has Clasps and straps for closing. The extra weight is heavy but manageable. She has had to leave some of her clothes behind to make room for the gold. She considers what to do with the dresses and sweaters and decides to bundle them up. She looks around for a box or anything that will hold clothes, there isn't anything in the cabin. She decides that it might look better if she leaves the extra clothes hanging in the cabins closet and hangs them up nice and neat. She has trouble Carrying the heavy leather suitcase and wishes for the two-wheel Carrier that the Captain used. She isn't a big woman and not at all strong, she weighs 95 pounds and is built for fun not a beast of burden. She decides to look around for a volunteer to help her, she can get most men to do whatever she wants. She opens the Dorr and steps out into the passage way, there's no one. The ship gets spooky when no one is aboard.

Nan comes back in the cabin and decides she will just have to slide the bag along and has to get down on hands and knees. She backs up pulling the bag by planting her knees and reaching the bag with her hands and jerking it towards herself. This Could take all day, or longer, if only she Could find a big guy. She Could use her sexual Charms to get the sucker to Carry her luggage. When she finally gets to the elevator, she is puffing hard and has to rest. She is very vulnerable and looks around. Still theirs no one, and she relaxes some. She thinks she could call a cab and ask the driver to carry her bag for her. She finds her phone and starts to call when a hand reaches around her and grabs her phone. She knows that Oder anywhere, it's Mr. Big or whatever his name is. Mr. Big,

"say Nannie or whatever your name is, where are you going?"

Nan turns almost white with fright, she had no idea that he was around, she tells him,

"hey baby, I was just getting my things and coming home to you."

Mr. Big wants to know why is that bag so heavy? She says,

"I don't think it's so heavy, I'm just small don't you know."

Mr. Big tells her that she should open up her suitcase and show him what's in there that's so heavy. Nan nearly faints, she didn't bargain for anything like this. She tries to shrug it off, she snuggles up to him attempting to change his mind with her very lovely small body. He doesn't need any more women; he gets more than he wants some times. He thinks he can just shove this little squirt down a sewer grate and the rain water will wash her away. He pushes her aside with one hand and lays the suitcase on its side. Nan gets really mad at being shoved around by this Creep and finds her nice little pearl handle pistol and pulls it out of her handbag. She has never killed anyone before but doesn't hesitate. Mr. Big feels something against the back of his head and stops. He doesn't know much about guns himself but realizes that the little bitch has a gun against his head. Nan is cool, and in a low voice full of menace says,

"you're a filthy animal, you stink, you're incredibly boring and I have my gun pointed at your very stupid head."

Nan is surprised herself at what she has said, she isn't a violent person, just a thief. Mr. Big knows he is in trouble; this little witch Can just pull the trigger and its lights out for him. He doesn't move, not a muscle, and in a shaky voice,

"nan dear, I was going to share with you, you're my favorite of course, the others don't matter."

Nan is young but not stupid, she knows a liar when she hears one. She utters an ugly laugh low in her throat, she likes this power over a big bruit like Mr. Pig here. She tells him to get down on his knees and try begging. Mr. Big doesn't like that at all, and gets mad but remembers her gun against his head. He folds to the Carpet on his knees. She stands off to the side, she realizes he can knock her over with a backward movement of his arm and maybe grab her gun or her. She reaches out with her extended arm placing the gun against the side of his head instead of the back. It doesn't matter, a bullet to the head is just as deadly no matter where the bullet goes in. She slowly moves around him never allowing the gun to lose contact with his head. She gets almost in front and has her gun over his left eye. She is a slight figure standing in front of Mr. Big, he knows he can still be killed by this mad woman. He decides she must be mad, to dare to point a gun at him. Nan isn't sure what to do next, she doesn't know many people here in the U.S. She needs help carrying the gold, and thinks again about a cab driver she Can hire. She wonders what to do with Mr. Biggs after she kills him witch she wants to do in the worse way. She decides to make him go back to the Captain's cabin, at least he will be out of sight for a while. She moves back behind him never losing Contact with his head with her gun. He wants to jump her but is terrified of that little gun, she makes him get up slowly and enters the elevator. She tells him to push the button for the sixth deck and up they go. The Captain's cabin isn't far from the elevator and she moves him back to the cabin. She tells him to lay on the floor, and when he is down on his belly, she kneels at his head. He follows orders laying on the thick Carpet, the Carpet is blue over darker blue like so much of this ship. Nan places her gun against the top of his head and pulls the trigger. She is surprised how simple it is, she just gave the trigger a little tug and bang he's dead. The caliber of her gun is small; she doesn't know what or care. The man jerks than is still. She doesn't know much about vital signs and doesn't want to touch a dead man so she shoots him again. She likes how that feels and keeps on shooting until the gun clicks empty. She is trying to remember how to put more bullets in her gun and looks at the extra's in her purse. There is one of those little things with all the extra bullets and she pulls it out. She has no idea how to reload her gun, or even how to get the old one out. She remembers to lock the cabin door and decides to take a quick look. She slams the door shut, the nasty bad guys that Mr. Big hires for beating people up are Coming off the elevator. They have seen her slamming the door and soon are pounding and shouting,

"hey bitch let us in or we will bust down this door."

Nan is frantic, and locks herself in the big bathroom. She is trying to remember how to put the new bullets in her gun. She is pushing on various parts of the weapon and it just drops out, the empty bullet thing drops on the floor. She is relieved but only for an instant, the cabin door Comes off its hinges, crashing onto the carpet. The big thugs look around and right away see Mr. Big laying on the carpet dead. They notice the locked bathroom door and bring out their own guns. These gentlemen aren't nice, they just open fire at the closed door. Nan is small and is sitting on the floor to the side of the door and they miss her. She has never been so terrified; the bullets are slamming into the opposite wall the sinks the mirror everything gets pulverized by dozens of bullets. They finally run dry and the shooting stops. The three bad guys don't know what to do next, their boss guy Can't tell them what to do. They simply take the comforter off the bed and roll Mr. Big up like a tortilla. They will give him the same treatment that Captain Martin got. They will put him in the trunk of the Ford and take him to the latest tree project and grind him up with the trees. The truck hauling Chips holds tons with a 20-foot box and two ground up bodies won't take up much space. Once the load is dumped at the land fill and Covered over no one will ever know that these two guys existed. The Chinese girl doesn't matter, they will simply get rid of their guns, they place them in wet Cement and drop them overboard in the ocean. What's another rock on the seabed? These guys aren't really bright but they do have experience. They are thinking of those little girls back at Mr. Biggs boat, and lick their lips in anticipation. They divide up and one goes to bring the Car Closer and one looks around the ship for strangers and the third carries the body over his shoulder. Mr. Big wasn't a big man, he isn't hard for this guy to carry. The entire job goes off without a hitch and Mr. Big gets installed in the large trunk

CHAPTER 44

At the headquarters building Joni and Joe are managing the business. Joni is not entirely comfortable in Carmen's place, there are questions she cannot answer. She admires Carmen for what she does and what she knows. Joni asks Joe often, and together they get by. A new girl is at the main desk on the first floor and is nervous. She Calls Joni often asking what seems to Joni to be simple questions. Joni is patient with her remembering what it was like for her at first. Joni picks up the ringing phone and knows its Jo Anne from the front desk,

"hey Jo what's happening now?"

"oh, Joni theirs a very angry man here, he says he is from the Kenneth Martin and is asking for Rose."

"what does he want with Rose?"

"he won't tell me, he is getting demanding, should I call security?"

"oh, no not yet, people just want to be heard, send him up with an escort please."

"ok thanks Joni."

The unhappy man is the first mate from Captain Martin's ship, he wants to know ware in the hell the lazy good for nothing Captain is. How Can he do his job if the bastard isn't around when he is needed. Joni, tries to Calm him down, she isn't as good at that as Carmen. Finally, she understands that there are responsibilities the Captain has to take care of and no one else can. Joni calls Rose on their satellite phones and tells her the situation. Rose has had problems like this before, and decides to ask Jones's opinion.

"how long has the first mate been with us?"

"he's been working on ships for most of his life, he is 27 years old and has a good record. He is up for being Captain in a few years."

"well I didn't get a good feeling with Captain Martin, but Jack really didn't like him, it is as if Jack new him from before. Usually when Jack reacts like that it's because he thinks the guy is a danger. We red through his papers and everything was in order, so we hired him. I trust your judgement of course and so if you think this first mate is ok than make him Captain for now."

"ok that's what I thought you would say, I just wanted to be sure."

Rose asks Joni to let her talk with the first mate, she is trying to remember his first name. She does remember that his last name is Winters. Rose says,

"Mr. Winters, I'm sorry I don't remember your first name, do you mind reminding me?"

Winters tells her that his first name is Randy, and Rose,

"of course, Randy now I remember, your dad worked for my father on one of our tugs, right?"

"yes Ms. Rose, he did, and I have always wanted to be a sailor too and here I am, thank you."

"Mr. Winters, we have a problem, we are in Georgia with a big mess, and so I need for you to take over Captain Martin's duties for now. When he returns, he had better have a good explanation, otherwise he is fired. If he isn't really sick or dead, he is history"

Randy Winters doesn't know what to say, he hardly knows Captain Martin, and he tells Rose that. She tells him that as of now he is in Charge of the Kenneth Martin and will please assume duties of Captain. She wants to talk with Joni please.

Joni has heard one side of the conversation but can guess the rest. Suddenly Mr. Winters isn't grumpy any more, he is sounding very satisfied. Rose,

"Joni, I need you to print out papers for Captain Winters there, and tell book keeping to increase his pay accordingly. Also, find him a Captain's uniform, there's not much difference but it will show Mr. Winters we are serious. Joni is elated with her new responsibilities and answers, "yes mam, right away."

Rose Can understand Joni's feeling of being asked to do more. Joni has some self-doubts she needs to get over, she is intelligent and Rose will keep asking more until Joni reaches her potential. Joni has to ask Joe what she should do, she isn't totally sure, she knows but doesn't know. Joe is happy for his friend and comes over to help her. Joe knows what Rose wants and tells Joni what to do, he won't do her job for her. Joni is sitting at Carmen's desk and uses the computer with voice over. She is nervous and makes some typing mistakes but back space fixes everything. After she has Captain Winters finished, she leans back in Carmen's Chair and realizes with a start that she hasn't thought about Don for a long while now. She doesn't forget him, but he's not in the front of her mind either. She tells Joe that she is grateful for his help. Joe shrugs it off, saying that she did all the work. He also tells her that she looks happy and pretty too. Joni hasn't thought about how she looks for a long while and smiles a big smile at Joe."

CHAPTER 45

Nan is surprised she is still alive, how many bullets came through that door. She for once is grateful that she is so small. She pasted herself to the floor rolling away from the door as far as she could. She has some ringing in her ears, those guns were really loud. She doesn't move for a long, long, time, and when she can hear again, she listens but hears nothing. She finally dares to crack open the door, it's not much of a door any more. The gun shots have punched out all of the wood in the Center only the edge is standing. She wonders why the Creeps didn't bother looking inside the room for her. She guesses those guys aren't really smart, and then she notices that Mr. Biggs is gone. She realizes that they were more worried about being found out with a dead body amongst them. She looks around and finds only what she left behind when she first left the cabin. She opens the hallway door and peaks out. The passageway is empty, nothing or no one there. She finally remembers how to load her little gun and is satisfied with the snick when she seats the clip. She moves down the hallway to the elevator, and with a shaky finger pushes the button. The elevator comes up to her floor and when the doors opens, she sees the catsup on the floor and some on the walls too. She doesn't use catsup at home but knows what it is only because Mr. Nice puts it on everything. She has her gun in both hands and pushes the button with the end of the barrel. The elevator arrives on the main deck and there is her leather suitcase laying on its side. She pushes it with her foot and is for once happy to feel its weight. The thugs walked right past it, not knowing what was inside. She still has her original problem, what to do about moving something that is too heavy for her. She finds her phone and calls for a cab, and in just a few minutes one pulls up to the ship. There must be cabs floating around all the time, waiting for her to call. She uses her best and sexiest voice and she hopes looks innocent, to get the guy to carry her suitcase for her. The man isn't big but strong and lifts it with ease. He places her bag in the trunk and opens the door for her. She is thinking this is more like it, what I deserve. Nan tells him she wants to go to the nicest hotel he knows, away from the water if he knows of one. The man is from Pakistan and has terrible breath, he smells like Currie and Garlick, his teeth are broken and rotten and she can smell his breath even when he isn't facing her. She plays her part well showing him that he is the most important man in the world. He drives to the hotel she wants and offers to help her to the front desk. She accepts with grace and even takes his arm for a bit. The guy is smiling like a jack'-o-lantern broadcasting more of that bad breath. She is tough and does her best to ignore him. She uses one of her fake names and offers a passport in the name of Kim Change. She has no idea who Kim Change is, or even if she exists it doesn't matter, she pays in Cash anyway. She gives the Cabby fifty dollars, that is much more than the meter indicates but she is feeling expansive. She gets a room on the twenty-fifth floor and engages a bell boy to carry her bags. The man leads her over to a bank of elevators and holds the door for her. She gets settled in and right away orders room service, she has several hundreds of dollars from some ware probably Captain Martin.

CHAPTER 46

Jones and Rose are requested to talk with the local police yet again, Jones hates the cops. Rose hasn't been grilled before like Jones has and is terrified. Jones won't let them separate him from Rose. Theirs's a difference of opinion and finally the cops shrug and invite them into a small room. There is the usual table bolted down to the floor and block walls that are painted green. The Chairs are the folding kind and Can't be more uncomfortable. Jones doesn't know what happened to Carmen and Braidy, he can only hope they are ok. The police aren't bad this time, they have no reason to suspect them of anything. They are asking general questions that seems right, and finally he and Rose are calmer. Rose shows her information to the cop who looks just plane board. He is impressed that she owns Big Lift Shipping and salvage and Lumber. He has heard of her of course, and knows that the lumber company has added a lot to the local economy He, like others, believes the camps burning down was an unfortunate accident. He tells them they can go after getting the information. Braidy and Carmen are waiting for them outside the building and they decide to wave down a Cab. They need to rest and tell the driver to take them to a hotel. The one that Comes to mind first is an Embassy Suites. Braidy and Carmen are not shy and just decide to get a room with two beds. Rose and Jones need only one. Braidy although upset after the excitement is still hungry. Even Carmen decides she is too and off they go for food

CHAPTER 47

Captain Randy Winters knows the ship and doesn't have to do much moving. His Cabin isn't far from the Captain's Cabin and when he gets there is shocked to see all the bullet holes in the bathroom door and opposite wall. He Can still smell the Cordite from the gunfire. He doesn't know what to do, and finally decides to Call Joni. When she answers the phone, she is also shocked. She didn't count on anything like this with her new acquired responsibilities. She finds Joe and tells him what Captain Winters has told her. Joe decides to find Nancy and when he does tells her the situation. Nancy is patrolling around the building with Jack and comes up to the office on the private elevator. Joe says,

"hey Nancy, Joni has something she needs to tell you."

"well Nancy, I helped Randy Winters get set up as Captain of the Kenneth Martin and he tells me that Captain's Cabin is full of bullet holes. Nancy says,

"oh shit, not more crap!"

Nancy Calls the security office and tells them to round up everyone in security. There are 30 people working in security now and most are big guys with lots of muscles. The guys work out often and can defend themselves well. They have set up a firing range behind the hanger building and go there often. They are all good marksman and just don't miss much. She tells Joe and Joni that she and 8 guys will fly down to San Diego. She calls Mac at the hanger and tells him to get a King Air ready. Mac tells her that they're both gone, one with Braidy and one with Jones. Nancy has forgotten about the planes both being gone. There are three planes left in the hanger, a Cessna 180 Brady's float plane, and a Beech Craft Bonanza. The Bonanza

Carries 6 and the Cessna 4. So, 10 security people Can go. Nancy doesn't feel comfortable using unknown hirelings. She doesn't know what they will find there. She thinks who else Could fly, and there's no one just her. There aren't so many people wanting to learn to fly lately. Nancy remembers that Barbra and asks Joe what he thinks. Joe,

"well I don't know her very well; she keeps Calling here asking for that Braidy fellow. I tell her that he is busy like he said to say. Nancy,

"do we have a number where she can be reached? Yes, we do it's on the caller ID. Nancy reviews her guys and decides to go with 9. These guys are all experienced and can work together. She calls security and tells the office woman to call her people. The security is spread all over the building and other places too and getting them gathered takes a while. She decides to meet in Roses office, and Joni and Joe can listen in as well. She tells them that they need to fly down to San Diego ware the ship is docked and investigate. They all gather up their equipment and drive out to the hanger. Barbra is excited to be useful and is waiting on the dock after driving her faster boat to the shore. She is dressed in jeans this time, with her hair tied back and out of the way. Her hair is very long reaching to her knees and is heavy and full. She piles it up under a baseball cap. The Caps says New York Yankees on the front. She has her father's revolver in her purse, and Nancy sees the purse sag down with extra weight. Nancy knows Barbra,

"oh, no you don't, you Can't do any shooting, you're only the airplane driver."

"oh, no mam, I always bring it on these dangerous missions."

Nancy knows that Barbra has flown one time to Los Angeles and says she has her eye on you, you Barbra girl you."

Mac and the guys have both aircraft ready, fueled and waiting. The Cessna is in front and Barbra and 3 big boys Climb aboard. She is feeling really important and opens the doors for everyone. She asks them to be oh so Careful with those big bad guns please. The guys are taken by this island girl and are all flirting with her. Barbra eats it all up and gives as much as she gets. She goes down the Check list like it was a bible verse. She starts the engine that roars to life, she has forgotten to retard the throttle first. She looks around but Braidy isn't there of course. Braidy always scolds her for starting an engine at full throttle. What dummy left the dam thing full on anyway. She gets a wave from Nancy who has started the Beech Crafts engine and is just waiting for Barbra. Nancy says on the radio,

"ok mam, you Can go if you would pleas."

"ok yes mam, Ms. Nancy with the pretty baby here I go."

They fly at 2000 feet, because of Jacks ear problem, they have squeezed him in with the five guys in the Bonanza. Nancy only hopes that Jacks tummy isn't riled up, she tries to remember what he has had to eat lately. She thinks he's good, Jack doesn't think he's good, he is half under the back seats and is miserable. He thinks he's getting too old for this stuff. Jack understands theirs some sort of Crisis but what else is new. He just does his job and puts up with it.

The two planes land at San Diego airport and the ten of them and Jack find ground transportation and rent two cars. They haven't told anyone they are coming and drive to the docks. The ship is being unloaded and is nearly empty. Nancy Calls Captain Winters on her satellite phone and he picks up right away. He sounds anxious and out of breath. Nancy tells him that she and 9 others are on the dock. Captain Winters comes down to the main deck and waves them on board. It's then he notices Jack and steps back in surprise. He exclaims,

"I have never seen a dog that big not ever."

Jack sits back on his but, and holds out his paw for shaking. Randy stoops down and takes it, saying,

"how do you do."

Nancy asks "Are you armed?",
"

Captain Winters tells her that he is, and he shows her his automatic he keeps in his belt. The guy is loaded Nancy sees, and she asks,

"do you know how to use that gun?"

Winters tells her that he is in the Coast Guard reserves and goes out on maneuvers every month. He tells her that small arms fire is included in their training. Nancy sees in his eyes that he has some sand in his Craw. She wonders where did that Come from, she must be hanging around Jones again. Are you the only one on board now?

Winters tells her that he is as far as he knows. She says,

"Can you show us the Cabin?"

Yes of course he answers and takes them over to the elevator. He opens the cabin door and right away they smell the cordite and see the ruined bathroom door. The Captain tells them that he will just stay in his old cabin for now. The Captain's Cabin will need to be repaired before anyone can use it. What happened here, they all want to know? Something that's for sure. Jack has been following along with the rest and comes to the spot on the floor ware Mr. Big had been laying. He looks at the spot than back at Nancy than back at the spot. This time he sniffs all around than moves over to the bathroom door. He looks in than back at Nancy. Nancy and Jack have worked together often and she understands that Jack is describing the seen in his own way. Nancy tells them,

"jack is good, I think he is telling us that someone was in the bathroom hiding probably when bad guys Came in. I don't understand the rest yet, only I believe there may have been a dead body on the floor there pointing at the spot where Mr. Biggs laid."

Jack barks once looking at her, and Nancy wants to tell him,

"good dog."

She refrains, and just nods at Jack. Jack is moving around the cabin sniffing and poking his nose into Corners. He stands at the closet door and looks back at Nancy, he wants her to open the door she thinks. Nancy gets it, and opens the door for him. Jack noses in and looks all around and up at the clothes rod. The closet is mostly empty but not entirely. There are women's clothing hanging there very neatly. Nancy sees that the clothes are for a very small woman, smaller than Carmen even. She adds this information to the collection. She thinks to herself, and is talking out loud. The others are out in the passageway and are examining other cabins too. They find not much just belongings that would belong to anyone working on this ship. Nancy remembers to ask, Captain Winters, What about all that catchup on the elevator?"

"I don't know, except that I know that Captain Martin always Carried a bottle like that with him."

Nancy wonders why anyone would do something like that. This Case gets stranger by the minute. They go back to the elevator looking all around. Jack sniffs at the Catsup on the Carpet and looks out to sea. Nancy thinks he is wondering too, she lays her hand on Jacks big noggin hoping she Can read his mind. No way theirs nothing but Jack fur beneath her hand. Jack leans up against her leg joining them together at least physically. Nancy decides to go over everything again. She needs a big board or some paper to make a flow Chart like Ken used to. She knows that Rose hates her father at least what he was responsible for but still the method worked for her. how did that catsup end up on the elevator floor? No one knows, even Jack just looks away meaning he has no idea either. Jack sniffs around the elevator avoiding the Catsup and looking up at Nancy. She comes over to him kneeling down beside him and gets her nose close to the carpet. She finds nothing, just very thick carpet. She stands back up and asks,

"Captain "Winters, do you have a large piece of paper, something we Can use for a flow chart?"

He answers yes of course, and they Can use the big conference room on the bridge level. They push the button and rise up to the bridge. There is a conference room with 12 Chairs around and even a large screen for projecting videos on. The Captain produces an old chart, the back is empty and Nancy Can use it for what she wants. She finds books that are heavy enough to hold down the Corners. She looks around and Captain Winters brings markers they use for marking charts with. Nancy starts out with the date and the location on what she calls the top. She lists all the people that are present and gives labels to the ones who are not. She calls the dead body on the cabin floor Mr. X with a question mark. She calls the one who may have been in the bathroom the mouse. The one who may have been in the elevator Mr. Heinz for catsup.

Nancy remembers well and list people and possible events in nice Columns. She doesn't like what Ken was responsible for, but he was her boss for years. She liked him as a person, he was always polite and treated her with respect. Nancy doesn't forget that he hired her when being black was a crime not a skin Color. She feels better after writing everything down and in order. She explains to the others what she is doing and why. The new guys in security are impressed with their boss, they think she has created the idea on her own. Jack is not satisfied, he is walking all around the bridge, sniffing looking and she sees listening. He searches every ware and leaves nothing to chance. Jack moves out of the bridge and down the passageway towards the elevator. He Comes back to the conference room looks at Nancy than barks in her face. Nancy would be slightly pissed at that but knows Jack. She says,

"it looks like master Jack here has something to show us. Jack barks again. Jim,

"say Nancy does that dog understand English?"

Nancy says,

"well I think he does, at least he seems to understand some of us."

Jack leads them down the passageway to the elevator and looks at Nancy again. She gets it and pushes the button. The elevator arrives and she pushes the button for the main deck. Jack steps out ahead of everyone and heads for the gang plank, and looks back a Nancy. She looks over to the dock and sees nothing, she watches Jack. Jack looks at the dock than back at her and barks. Nancy,

"I'm sorry big boy I don't get it, what are you saying?"

Barbra who has mostly been forgotten says,

"hey dog, what's over there, what you seeing my big black friend?"

Jack looks at her with hope, and goes over and licks her hand. She says,

"hey dog you want me to follow you over on the shore?"

Jack barks at her and takes her sleeve tugging gently, Barbra follows along like she is the dog. Nancy tells some of her guys to wait on the ship, and she and one other go ashore with Jack and Barbra. Jack stops at the spot where the bad guys parks the Crown Vick. There is only Cement nothing Can be seen. Jack looks at the ship at Nancy than at the spot. Nancy finally gets it again and says, "someone parked a vehicle here? Jack barks. She says and I'll bet a body was loaded into the trunk or inside. Jack barks again. Barbra is amazed at Jack,

"hey dog, your one smart mutt."

Jack doesn't say a word, he goes further onto the dock, sniffing looking and Circling all around. What ever happened on the ship was apparently removed by a vehicle that was parked here. Jack Circles around again than moves back to the ship. He looks back at Nancy and lowers his big head, he has finished with whatever Caused him to explore more.

Nancy thinks all about what Jack has been doing and tried to order her thoughts, she will add this information that Jack has discovered to the Chart. She doesn't know what good anything she adds will actually do but she knows it will help in the end. When they get back to the conference room behind the bridge Captain offers them Coffee, there is a coffee maker in a small kitchenet at the end of the room. They are all comforted by the smell of Ken's favorite coffee blend and smile at each other. One guy says,

"it's just like home, if only we had some of those baked goods from around the Corner bakery. Jack lays in the corner with his head on his paws, he is either really tired or reflecting on today's events. Nancy knows that Jack is smarter than other dogs, but how smart. She remembers that Jones told them that Jack may have had some implants installed in his head like Jones, maybe those implants make him into a super dog.

CHAPTER 48

In Seattle Joe and Joni watch everyone leaving for the day, only some of Nancy's security people are left for the night watch. Joni is feeling lonely and wants to ask Joe if he would like to get a bite to eat? She hasn't been out on a date since that one time with Braidy. She likes Braidy but didn't have a good time, she was missing Don too much. She finally works up the nerve and burst out,

"hey Joe would you like to take me out for dinner?"

Joe stops locking the doors and turns to her,

"what did you say, dinner you say?"

Joni tells him that's what she said if he's not busy. Joes swallows hard, he was thinking the same thing. Neither one of them realize or seem to care that there is a 15-year age different. Joni has kept herself in good shape, working out some and walking a lot. She has offered to take good old Jack for long walks. Joe tells her,

"you know I was thinking the same thing, I just didn't think you would be interested. Joni,

"well I am interested you big dummy, now come on let's go please."

Joe takes her hand and asks,

"ware?"

Joni says anywhere except that little Italian restaurant, you know the one down the stairs at the end of the block.

Joe squeezes her hand and tells her that he understands. He will take them anywhere she likes; he has his car, and can drive them. Joni has thought about riding around in a car lately. She thinks what a novel idea, and says ok.

Joe and Joni drive to a quaint little Chinese restaurant that smells good. Chinese food is good once in a while, the trouble is for Joni is that after a few hours she's hungry again. Joe tells her that they always can find a fast food place if their still hungry. Joni is ok with that and says drive on please. She doesn't drive. They are walking down the sidewalk after finally finding a parking spot. She is thinking maybe driving isn't so great after all if you always have to find a place to store your car. They are seated by a pretty Chinese girl who is small. Joe wonders how old she is, but doesn't ask. Joni and Joe both remember the problem with the Chinese women from the container ship. They know that Rose managed to keep some of the women in the United States. She hired lawyers that are good but creative too. They didn't break the law only bent it slightly. This young lady happens to be one of those women that Rose rescued. She recognizes the uniform shirts they are waring and smiles big as all outdoors. She says,

"you work for my Rosy, right?"

Joni and Joe aren't sure what she is talking about, they look Confused. The girl tells them that she is one of the women that Rose helped after being shipped in that container thing. Joni finally gets it, and smiles back, saying,

"Yes, we do work for Rosy, and are happy about that."

Joe and Joni have a lot to talk about and chatter freely, and Joe thinks that Joni looks prettier every minute. She has a nice laugh and tells funny stories about people she has had to deal with at work. She is warm and funny and makes Joe feel happy. Joe hasn't been around the world that much; he is Hispanic and came from pore people. He likes working for Rose and is proud of his new responsibilities. Joni enjoys Joe too and wants to know more about him. After hours, they discover the restaurant is closing and they have to leave. Joe drives them back to headquarters building and Joni uses her key card to unlock the door. Joe offers to walk her up to her apartment and she accepts. She is hoping for a good night kiss. She gets off the elevator and slowly walks to her door, and Joe is walking just as slow. Joni unlocks her door and turns to him, he is shy. Joe, touches her hand and she takes his hand. They just come together easily naturally. They share a tender kiss that both will remember for probably always. Joe is embarrassed and says,

"Well Joni, I really enjoyed being with you tonight, do you thing we Could do that again?"

Joni, can hardly speak and when she finally does, says,

"I hope so, I enjoyed it too, you're really nice and I like being with you."

CHAPTER 49

In Georgia, the four friends are trying to enjoy a nice dinner, however it turns out to be a very expensive Atlanta restaurant. Braidy and Carmen are still shaken by what happen at the camp. Rose and Jones sit a Crossed the table holding hands and listening to both of them. Carmen,

"I wasn't very hungry, I don't always feel like eating, and slipped out to the kitchen for a cup of private coffee. The cook was coming in and out, and offered me some homemade pie. I wasn't hungry and sort of picked at it. The coffee was all I wanted, it was the usual blend we all like. The cook didn't sound like a black lady, even though Braidy here said she was. She was moving very easily like she was much younger than her age should allow. She didn't Complain like people with arthritis usually do, she just didn't feel right to me. I can't always depend on what I'm hearing though. Maybe I was mistaken, I want to give everyone the benefit of the doubt. I did enjoy the coffee fixed just like I like it, you know with lots of creamer. Rose smiles at her friend remembering. Carmen continues, everyone finished eating including Jaws here bumping Braidy with her small fist. Braidy has been watching her and says,

"ouch, that hurt, quit that you big bully."

Carmen tells them that they went outside after lunch to watch the poles being installed. She says that Braidy was complaining of being tired and heard the boom truck moving the pole. She heard guys screaming when the pole slammed into them. I just climbed on top of Braidy here and made him wake up. I kept on poking him and shouting in his ear until he woke up. Braidy,

"Finally, a pretty woman takes advantage of me and I'm down for the count, it just isn't fare I tell you."

Carmen delivers another mighty Munchkin punch from her fists and goes on. When I got Braidy here to come back to life he suggested that we run to the rental car. Just then someone set the car on fire, I heard a big whoosh and then smelled smoke. Braidy than told me about the machine shed, and we ran over there. There wasn't anything in there except a bull-dozer. Braidy got me into the Cab and squashed me down behind the seat. Four bad guys showed up in front of us with guns and so good old Braidy here drove us out of there. The cook who wasn't the cook, had a shot-gun and shot at us but didn't do any damage. When we got outside facing the bad guys, they just stepped aside and let us pass. After climbing into the boom truck, Braidy drove us out, and you know the rest.

Rose takes her hand and reassures Carmen that she did good, they both did. Braidy chases a wayward shrimp around Carmen's plate with his fork. Carmen grabs his big wrist with both her small paws and says,

"Stop that you thief, I was saving that one for dessert."

Braidy gulps it down and tells her that she's too late. She smacks him yet again on his arm, he again says ouch.

Rose tells them that this will cost them this time, the insurance won't cover anything, they don't say why and she will get the lawyers on it. Jones thinks he knows and explains,

"You know that Braidy and I were here last year or so. We discovered some discrimination going on out in the woods. I think that some folks haven't forgotten that and have retaliated. They targeted the camp using poisoned food to kill everyone or knock them out then finish the job by burning the camp down. The accident with the boom truck was not planned. The cook was no doubt killed by one of them and that other woman that Carmen noticed wasn't really real did the deed. The other four guys Could be anyone, say Braidy,

"I don't suppose you could tell if those guys were wearing some sort of masks, do you?"

Braidy shakes his head no, I was trying to keep Ms. Carmen and I from being killed with the rest."

Jones asks,

"Do we know how many workers were black?"

Rose answers,

"Oh, that's easy of course all of them who worked for us were black." Remember we agreed to hire only black people to work at the camp because of what happened?"

Jones asks,

"Could either one of you tell if the guys working on the powerline, were black?"

Braidy tells them that yes, they all were black folks there were only three of them.

Jones continues,

"So, if everyone working at the camp and for the power company were black than I think we're right, it was definitely a hate crime. Rose is just sick hearing that, what in the hell difference does it make if someone is black or not. She wishes sometimes she Could get mad or whatever Jones does and just smash those assholes into paste. She looks at Jones feeling a little guilty. Jones looks back at her with a question. Rose wants to ask but hasn't got the nerve. Finally, she does,

"Say Jonesy, how do you get mad enough to smash heads, and could you show me how?"

Jones leans over and kisses her very pretty soft lips and says,

"It's a man's job to smash heads don't you know." Braidy Complains,

"Well I'm a man, how Come I can't smash heads like you do?"

Jones, admits he doesn't know, but we Could get some water-melons and practice with sledge hammers. Rose kisses him back and snuggles in Closer. Braidy loves Carmen but wishes for Barbra. Carmen doesn't miss a thing and says,

"And you Mr. Braidy just be watching yourself, I will know what you ben up to over there in that Georgia place."

Braidy looks around at all the plates, after all someone may have missed something. Too bad, all plates bowls glasses cups are all empty, clean as a whistle.

Carmen just has to, she puts her hands around Brady's arm laying her Cheek against him and gently squeezes. Braidy puts his arm around her and pulls her in close. He knows that Carmen is just needing comfort, she isn't as tough as she thinks some times. Braidy is feeling fatherly and puts his Cheek on the top of her pretty head smelling shampoo, sweat old perfume and smoke. Hair can really tell a tall tale if you sniff just right. Carmen is feeling sleepy and says she needs to get some sleep. Jones and Rose agree and Jones gathers up the bill. He looks at it than hides it from Rose. He says it's not acceptable material for a lady. Rose says she doesn't care, they have money they haven't spent yet. Jones doesn't care either even though the bill was over $200. Jones has forgotten the tip again and this time Braidy pulls out a fifty placing it beneath the napkin holder. He thinks that the wait staff shouldn't have to be paid by customers but keeps quiet

They decide there is nothing they can do at the logging camp. What will happen is up to the law this time, the company can't be held responsible for what happened. The company will probably have to absorbed the losses in land and equipment, the loss of life is a different story. Rose has records of all employees and will contact each family herself. She will settle with each family in her own way, no matter what the insurance company does. Rose thinks about little things and wonders if she should try and visit families after a while. She and Jones are flying back to Seattle followed by Braidy and Carmen. They look really nice Rose notices both these shiny planes one after the other. After what seems like too long, they finally arrive at the company strip. Its late afternoon and for once the skies aren't cloudy. The guys are mostly doing nothing, all the planes except for Brady's float plane and the helicopter are gone. Jones shuts down the King Air and helps Rose down the steps. Rose doesn't need any help but excepts it graciously. She waves at her mechanics and takes Jones's hand. Braidy and Carmen touch down and the smiles are huge on the mechanics faces. At last they will have some work to do. Braidy helps Carmen down the steps, except she doesn't need any help. She leaps into his arms, and holds on for dear life. Braidy,

"Carmen, what in the hell are you doing?"

Carmen,

"I'm sorry Mr. Braidy sir, I have always wanted to do that, did I hurt you?"

Braidy can't stay mad at her even for an instant and tells her nah it was nothing. Braidy is wondering where Barbra is, she is usually here to meet him,

"Say Mac, have you seen that Barbra around here?"

Mac,

"Well you see Mr. Braidy fellow; she went flying off in the Cessna with a bunch of handsome guys for San Diego."

Rose looks up,

"What are you talking about Mac? Do you mean she flew off by herself?"

Mac tells her that Nancy and another bunch of guys took the Bonanza. Rose wants to know why?

Mac,

"Well you see mam I'm just the airplane fixer, they don't always explain things to me, and well they didn't ask my permission either."

Rose pulls out her satellite phone and speed dials Nancy's number.

Nancy answers right away,

"Hello Rose, we're alright, no one is hurt, we will fly back in the morning. I can tell you all about it then if that's ok."

Rose leans up against Jones and sighs, she says,

"Let's go home ok?"

CHAPTER 50

Nancy and her guys have got nothing to do, if they report the gunshots to the police they could be there forever. The Dorr has been replaced and the bullet holes in the wall have been covered over with very nice paneling, and the vanity including fixtures are all new. Nancy thinks Rose will throw a fit when she gets that bill. Captain Winters is good, he has organized the crew and gotten them all on board ready for the next trip. The crew have known him for years and are glad he is their Captain. Nancy brings the rolled-up paper that they were using for the flow Chart. She doesn't know why; she just thinks she might need it. Nancy is satisfied with Captain Winters he is a no non-Cents kind of guy and takes charge with ease. The truth is, he has been conning the ship anyway, Captain Martin didn't know a ship from a hockey puck. The crew are efficient and one man short won't make any difference. The ship leaves with the morning tide and the security team Jack and Barbra watch them sail off. Nancy herds them all into the two cars and they drive back to the airport. She asks Barbra if she has ever flown the Bonanza before? Barbra tells her no not yet. Nancy decides that now isn't the time, she thinks Barbra could do it ok but why chance it, there is just enough difference to make it hard for her. Nancy pets Jack gently,

"I'm sorry old dog, you're going to have to ride in the back again."

Jack this time lifts his hind leg and roars out with a big long loud stinky gaseous Cloud that turns the air blue. Nancy steps back in horror exclaiming,

"I surrender."

The guys have heard of Jacks nasty fart making and hold their noses while laughing their heads off. Jack doesn't know a thing, he is after all just a dog, how can a dog understand words that people say.

The two planes make it back to Seattle and are greeted by Mac and the gang, at last they have all their charges back under the same roof. Joe is there waiting with a big van to hall everyone back to headquarters building. Braidy is there to in his Black truck. He watches Barbra touch down and admires the landing. From ware, he stands it looks good. Barbra stops near as she Can to Braidy and shuts down the plane rather quickly at least to Brady's mind. She leaps out running over to him, she grabs her man and pulls him close with a giant hug. Braidy says he can hardly breathe, loosen up woman. Barbra,

"Oh Mr. Braidy sir, I have missed you so very much, and I wasn't sure where you had got yourself too."

Braidy,

"Well what about you dashing all over the country without telling me."

Barbra,

"Oh, that Nancy woman made me do it sir, she told me that if I wanted to see you again, I had to fly her silly airplane a way down there to that San Diego place."

Nancy shakes her head at Braidy waving Barbra's Comments away like flies.

CHAPTER 51

A man named Cookie who saved a black guy named John-John from a gang of KKK Creeps reads all about the fire at his old camp. He doesn't like people who hate black guys. He has been taking care of himself. He is 68 years old and runs five miles, well walking the last two but still. He knows who is responsible for the big fire that killed 17 black folks at the logging Camp. He has a plan for revenge. No one knows that his mother was a black woman and he has never forgotten how much she loved him. He Can pass for white and does, but his heart is really black. He remembers knocking down those white guys in the Clearing in the woods and smiles to himself. They will never catch him he knows; he lives a quiet life and keeps all his personal information to himself. He uses a P.O. box and rents a room. He has no vehicle only renting an old pickup from a friend once in a while. He does receive Social Security and has it directly deposited in a bank in another town. He has kept himself out of sight out of mind. Cookie has no family anymore and misses talking to others. He has a bird that makes noises like folks do, but the bird isn't intelligent he doesn't think.

Cookie knows the man who is responsible for the latest fire and the earlier assaults. The man is a judge, a big man in the legal community, he isn't at all fare of course. Black men always get the maximum sentences no matter if the case is solid or not. The judge lives in Atlanta in a very impressive house. Cookie will get that judge if it's the last thing he ever does. Cookie knows he Can't let his emotions get in the way of logic. He makes plans and some are good but most are bad. He wants to get away with killing this very bad man. He doesn't care that much about his own life, after all those guys killed his mother for no reason. Maybe it wasn't the judge but it was people like him. Cookie has visited the judges house and seen him out in his garden. The garden Certainly wasn't used for growing anything for people to eat, just lots of those fancy flowers and bushes. The swimming pool is oh so nice too. Cookie doesn't know how to use a gun, they scare him to death. No not a gun, something else, something more painful would be better.

Cookie invents several plans, like running a broken power Cord into the swimming pool, a runaway riding lawn more, or one of those fancy Cars starting up on its own and running him over. Nothing stays formed, he has to make a better plan for this very special judge. Cookie has lost weight first because he wanted too but now, he's just not interested in food. He used to be a good Cook at least the loggers thought so, but their all gone now. The ones he is thinking of are the ones from a long time ago, before the new boss guys took over. He loved those boys, so hard working and yet so needy. They relied on him for almost everything. He wrote letters for some of them who Couldn't write and dug out slivers from others. He really liked helping those boys, and he misses them Those rough tough loggers were his family and he needed to be needed. Cookie has no family any more, he has out lived everyone. Cookie is looking through some old papers and Comes a Crossed a letter from the head office from someone named Rose, the letter is thanking him for years of service. Cookie is reminded of the two guys from Seattle and remembers how willing that one guy was to just sit and talk over coffee in the morning. The man's name was, maybe, oh yes Jones. The other guy's name was something, oh well it probably doesn't matter. The guy was so hungry and really tall. Cookie kept on feeding and feeding that guy and he still was hungry later. That boy must have had some sort of eating disorder. Cookie reads through Roses letter, he likes this woman's words, they say more than just words they express real meaning. Cookie wonders if that Rose still works for the big Company.

CHAPTER 52

In Seattle Nancy is explaining to Rose, Braidy, and Carmen what happened in San Diego. She tells them that she saw no reason to hold the ship. She has a good feeling about Captain Winters, and she believes that the men all like him. He knew all the right stuff when getting things in order, he apparently was doing most of the work anyway. I am beginning to think that Captain Martin may have been a fake. Rose Clears her throat meaningfully,

I beg your pardon, I'm the one who hired him, if you recall."

Nancy looks up at Rose and sees she is kidding. Nancy waves it off, of course you're right Rosy dear. Anyway, Captain Martin didn't know that much about container ships even though his records indicated he had years of experience. Jones says,

"Let me look some more at that picture of Captain Martin please?"

Rose asks,

"What are you thinking Mr. Jones sir."

Jones places his hand on her thigh squeezing gently. Well Rose, something doesn't feel quite right to me about this guy. Do you remember that Jack was giving him the evil eye during the interview? Jack is lying beside Braidy, just in case he may need some help in the kitchen. Jack wolfs softly than lowering his head down to rest on his paws. Jones looks at his dog and says,

"Right!"

Jones continues, "Do we still have that drawing that Joe made of the bad guy we saw in San Diego? Was it San Diego, oh well ware ever it was the drawing that joe drew?"

Rose says, "Sure, we do, it's right over in the files here."

After Rose hands him the drawing he lays it beside the picture taken for Captain Martin's employment. Jones isn't an expert but sees some similarities in the shape of the face and the head. He asks,

"Is Joe around the building?"

Rose says he is, and calls him on the PA system. Joe comes rushing in after two minutes, he is out of breath saying he was over to the post office. Rose wants to ask him why he goes to the post office but waits.

Jones asks Joe if he thinks the two pictures, the drawing and the print out look like they could be the same man? I mean do you think the guy I described could have been wearing a mask? Joe,

"Well Mr. Jones, I only drew what you suggested, I of course wasn't there. It's possible you may have not noticed a mask in the excitement of the moment."

Jones asks Rose,

"Do you still have those video recordings of the kidnappings? Rose explains of course and goes after the recordings. She knows what he will ask for next and inserts the Card into a Computer. She scrolls through the images until she comes to the one he wants. She freezes it than prints it out in color of course. The printer is excellent and produces a good picture. She hands him the photo and he lays them all side by side. Joe is hovering over one shoulder and Nancy is over the other. Jones looks like he is covered in bodies. Rose stands back watching him studying the pictures he puts one beside another shuffling them around. Finally, he stands up and says,

"Here Joe, you look at these with your artist's eye."

Joe sits where Jones was sitting and puts the pictures one above the other. Jones wonders why, but just waits. Joe wants a magnifying glass, and Rose brings one over for him. Joe looks like a detective with a spy glass. He moves the print outs in all different directions, puts it down than looks again. Joe,

"Yes, I think these men Could be the same guy, you Can't really see a mask but the nose and eyes don't look as distinguished as the open-faced picture. The difference is subtle, and that mask is really good but it's a mask alright. I'd say that the picture of Captain Martin is the real guy. Nancy says she wants to show the picture of Captain

Martin to her police contact. Jones doesn't like that; he wonders if they can eliminate the uniform first. Joe knows about pictures and says oh sure Photo Shop can crop out the uniform easy. Jones hasn't a clue what he is talking about, and Rose asks if they have one of those Photo Shops? Joe waves them off and says he will be right back.

Joe is true to his word; he comes breezing in the office with a Cup of coffee in one hand and a bag of still warm doughnuts in the other. Jack comes to life, his nose is working overtime, capturing that rich wonderful doughnut flavor. Joe didn't run to the doughnut-shop, he swiped the bag off of Joni's desk. She will probably be really mad when she returns from the lady's room. Joe gives Jones the picture and says he has to get back down stairs before Joni misses the pastries. Jones offers the cropped photo to Nancy and she says

"That will do nicely, thank you."

Jones is willing to bet the farm that the guy in the first drawing and the man in the second are indeed the same ones.

CHAPTER 53

Cookie thinks he has a working plan and sets about making it happen. He will learn how to make a bomb from the internet. The bomb will do much more than just kill the judge; it will get all the crooked prosecutors as well. The Court house not only has Court rooms but the prosecutors are there too. One bomb for all those bad guys, what a thrill. He knows what to do now, and searches on his computer. Cookie isn't too old to learn; he has a used computer several years old but very functional. Cookie doesn't understand all the meanings of what he reads on the screen but he gets most of it. The only problem is, he needs a credit card to purchase goods online. Well ok, he can get one, he will use his given name. Anyone who knows him won't recognize his real name, they just know him as Cookie. Besides isn't everything online supposed to be confidential Cookie doesn't believe that of course and decides to think some more. He doesn't want to get caught; he wants to be around to watch that big bad building blow up into rubble.

Cookie looks at dynamite, Plastique's, C4 and others, the words don't mean much to him, he has little or no experience with things that go boom. Cookie writes himself notes and keeps track of websites by time and dates he viewed them. The computer probably tells him these things but he still isn't use to using it yet. Cookie for the first time in a long while feels hunger pangs. He decides to visit a nearby café he likes ok, at least they have pretty good coffee. He remembers that coffee they had at camp, man oh man was that stuff ever good. They brought it in from some ware he doesn't know where he just knows it was so good! Cookie is greeted by a good-looking waitress, she knows his name and says,

"Hey Cookie, are you looking for a job, I hear you are a really good cook

Cookie remembers her name at the last instant and says,

"Hey Mable, how you doing, nope I don't want to cook any more, thanks though."

Mable holds a chair for him and he is smiling at her. He Can feel his face stretching funny like, he hasn't used any of those smiling muscles for a long while. Mable is ready standing there looking nice. Cookie admires her figure, and she notices,

"what are you looking at you silly old fool, I'm not worth looking at."

Cookie looks away quickly, he is embarrassed, he hasn't looked at a woman that way for at least 20 years or more. Cookie asks her what's good today? Mable says everything is good, but if I were you, I'd try the meat loaf. After all its fresh, todays road kill. Mable thinks that's so funny and howls with laughter. Cookie doesn't like howling women and studies the menu. He decides on spaghetti without meatballs please. He sees that there is pie under the counter behind glass. He asks,

"Is that pie strawberry?"

Mable admits that it is and that's the last piece. Cookie tells her that he wants it please

Cookie reads in the paper that the Court house is needing to hire a custodian. He sees some real possibilities and decides to apply. He will have to think about how to keep his real name off the application. Doing custodial work is nothing in a building like that, you just shove big dust mops around and clean the toilets. Cookie has found a source on the internet that will create fake documents and gets one made up for himself. He admires his picture; he doesn't look too bad for an old duffer. Mable at the Café says he doesn't look 70 years' young. He doesn't have much hair loss, just some on the top. He has lost about 40 pounds since Cooking at the logging Camp. If Mable thinks he looks younger than maybe the folks that hire custodians will too. He lists his age as 64 on his fake I D and thinks he Can pass for that. If he Can get hired as a custodian, he should be able to get in all the offices and Can take his time planting whatever device he decides on. He has been searching various web-sites and has found sources for some very nasty surprises. He is spending time educating himself on how explosives work. He doesn't want the killers to die so quickly though, rather he wants them to have to suffer. He has time to research and will apply for the job first.

CHAPTER 54

Rose is following the progress of her ships especially the Kenneth Martin. The shipping of containers is turning out to be a good investment. The return on the Cost of ships they have had built is good, more than she hoped for. Rose likes simple things like spending time with her roses or being with Jones. She enjoys her second Cup of Coffee amongst her roses with Jones and Jack. Jones likes to admire each rose bending down and sniffing. He settles in a lawn Chair beside the bubbling water feature stretching out his legs and sipping Coffee. She looks at him and thinks she is the luckiest woman on earth. Jones looks back and likes what he sees.

Carmen is making decisions about logging and lumber that cost millions, she is still young. She uses her computer and smart phones with ease now rarely ever needing sighted assistance. She communicates with Camp bosses, buyers, and then arranges shipping. She brings in millions of dollars in revenue monthly and is confident in everything she does. At first Rose was supervising her often but not lately. Carmen has become her best manager. Rose is starting to like having some time to play amongst her roses and she also enjoys long walks with Jones and Jack.

Joni is still working at the front desk, anyone who comes to the company has to get past her. She does her job well, screening out the Common problems and resolving many issues before they ever get to Carmen or Rose. Joni and Joe have been dating often and she is looking happier. Joe is practically glowing around the building. He is becoming more responsible. He has several duties including contracting with manufacturers who need to ship containers full of their products. Joe is full of energy and uses his intelligence and boyish

Charm to influence companies to ship on Roses ships. Joe lives in his parents' house; he helps them with appointments and grocery shopping. He can afford his own place of course but stays at home to help

Joe has his own office near Jones's and they share a secretary. Joe and Jones often share ideas about marketing and shipping. Jones admires Joe's good looks and vigor. Joe runs daily and works out in the gym. Jones is supposed to manage Joe's work but doesn't bother any more. Joe is confident and capable and Jones visits him just to be sociable. Joe receives a call from a shipper in China. The manufacturer doesn't have enough containers to ship all of his product. Joe stays cool asking about the container ship that is there to carry the containers after being filled with products. The shipper says there is no ship and no containers either. Joe remembers that the container ship left from Los Angeles and should have been there in China days ago, Joe looks at an electronic map displaying the positions of all their ships. The Kenneth Martin is there right where it should be. Joe is confused and tells the caller that he will have to get back to him. Joe goes to Jones and asks,

"Hey Jonesy, do you have time to discuss a problem?"

Jones,

"No, I don't want any more problems, I don't mind issues but no problems please."

Joe is amused and Jones sees that, he says,

"Sorry Joe, what you got?"

Joe tells Jones about the missing containers, and the map showing the position of their ship. Jones asks if he has tried to contact Captain Winters? Joe looks a bit foolish and says,

"What a novel idea, I tried that but no answer on the satellite phone or ships radios. Jones says,

"Oh, hell what next, ok I guess we better have a meeting with Carmen and Rose and try to find out what's going on."

Jones and Joe rise up to the upper office using the private elevator and tell the office man sitting at the outer office desk that they need to see Rose. This young man is tall and slim and very blond. He looks like he might be 14 maybe. Still he does his job, he is polite and asks them if they would like to sit down please? Jones and Joe are impressed and sit down. The guy's name is Jamie, and Jones thinks, is that really a guy's name. What's in a name. Jamie calls Carmen using the intercom and they hear Carmen answering. She says she hasn't got time for a couple of rogues like Jones and Joe. Jamie knows kidding when he hears it and says,

"Excuse me mam, but they are both bigger than me, and I'm not paid to get beat up you know."

Carmen sighs and tells him to send them in she will deal with tough guys, don't worry about it. Jamie snickers and tells the men to go on in please. He even gets up and holds the door open for them. Jones thinks at least this boy knows his manners

Rose is wearing a pretty blue over darker blue dress that Comes to the top of her knees. Jones admires her legs and starts to whistle but restrains himself. After all they aren't alone. Rose fills out the dress nicely, she has a beautiful full figure. Rose comes over to him giving her man a little quick hug and smiles at Joe. Carmen gets taller after standing up behind her desk. She has that silly platform that raises her 3 inches. Jones thinks it's silly but Rose thinks it's a good idea. First impressions are so very important. When Carmen steps down onto the Carpet she appears to get shorter, she steps down so gracefully. Carmen has a way of walking that makes her seem to glide rather than walking. She doesn't use a cane in the office, she knows every corner and doesn't need one. Jones and Joe tell the women about the mystery and they all gather at the stone table under the windows overlooking the harbor. They sit at one end of the big table; it is large enough for 12 people. Rose sits at the end, and Carmen is on her left. Jack comes awake and joins in the fun. Jones and Joe sit on either side of the table close to the end. Joe lays out the problem and Rose Sighs and says,

"I don't know if the name of a ship has anything to do with its travels but that ship has been a pain in the but ever since it was built. Carmen,

"Oh yes, that was the ship damaged when I broke the bottle of sham pain over the bough."

Rose says,

"Well that didn't have anything to do with you, you were just the bottle breaker."

Jones, tells them the bad guy is alive and well but probably not so happy living on that private island with good old Kenny."

I watched him earlier this morning with Nancy on a video feed and both the bad boys were just sitting around doing not much."

Rose sighs again,

"Well at least we don't have to worry about those two, right?"

Jones tells her that if they try to leave there for any reason, they will lose a foot when the collar blows up. She is alarmed and looks at him,

"Do I want to hear how that is possible?"

"No, you don't, just trust me they'll never leave that island, not alive that is."

CHAPTER 55

Cookie gets the job, working as custodian in the Court house. There wasn't much competition, no one really likes cleaning bathrooms and mopping floors all night. He gets right into it, and pleases his supervisor. He doesn't need a lot of training even though the boss guy says he does. Cookie is agreeable and says yes sir and no sir with regularity. He makes a good impression thinking the black part of him knows how to be submissive. Cookie doesn't look like a black man at least the part of him that shows to the public. Under Neath his shirt though he has a big dark brown spot. He feels like he is a black man and is proud of his heritage. He remembers details of the judge's chambers and the prosecutor's office. The plan is coming together, there's not a problem getting the explosives in the building. There are no security checks for Janitors coming to clean toilets. He can just walk in there Carrying his large lunch box. That lunch box can contain enough explosive material to send the entire building into orbit. He needs to work on getting out of town unnoticed and far away. Cookie remembers the letter from that woman Rose and wonders if he could get a job as cook on one of her ships. He decides to write her a letter asking just that. He doubts she will remember him but that tall guy will. What was his name, he tries to think, the guys face is right there but the name isn't? Oh well sooner or later he will think of it.

CHAPTER 56

The mail comes around the building twice a day and more if something extra comes. The mail carrier is a happy go lucky guy that Rose hired personally. Gerry is disabled, he has a cognitive disorder. Gerry can memorize what he needs to do and pushes the mail cart all around the building with ease. He can read, and sorts out the mail according to office, name and department. He is always cheery and likes to tell goofy jokes that most have heard before. He is a good-looking man and does his job well. Rose likes to hire as many different types of people as possible. They're deaf people working in shipping and packing and Gerry in mail delivery. Gerry brings a letter addressed to Rose from Georgia; Gerry is happy to deliver anything to Rose. Rose is funny and he tells her his latest goofy joke. Rose is polite and laughs at his funnies. Gerry pets Jack says hello to Ms. Carmen and waves them all good bye.

Rose doesn't remember anyone named Cookie, and sits down at her desk to read the letter. The letter has a copy of a letter she wrote years ago, when her father was in charge.

"Dear Ms. Rose, I used to work at your logging camp in Georgia. I am sorry to remind you that the camp has recently been burned to the ground. I am most sorry for the loss of lives. Ms. Rose mam, I am the man who cooked for the camp while Mr. Harvey was the boss. I am looking for something different now. To be straight forward I would like to ask you to consider me for a cooking job on one of your ships. I am in good health and will celebrate my 65th birthday in two months. I would like to see the world some before I retire. I have 25 years' experience as a cook and can cook for large or small numbers of people. I can prepare hardy meals or fancy food too. I think you may find my records in your older files but if not, you may tell me if you need new ones. Once again thank you for the very kind letter, and I am sorry for the loss of those folks at the logging camp. Yours Cookie!"

Rose doesn't handle hiring of cooks any more, there are people who do that now. She tries to think who does that and has to ask Carmen. She asks,

"Hey Carmen who hires ships cooks for us these days?"

Carmen tells her that she does thank you very much, what's up? Rose reads Cookies letter for her. Carmen tells rose she remembers; he was the guy that ran down those bad boys that were ready to roast Mr. John-John. Rose than remembers too,

"Oh yes, he's the one who disappeared after saving John John from the mob. We have always wondered where he got to after all that. We wanted to thank him, and Braidy and Jones were worried about him.

Rose is such a softy and will find this nice old gentleman a job somewhere on one of her ships. She uses a young lady from the secretary pool to dictate letters to, Rose can get more done that way. The young lady is a big woman about as round as she is tall. She is efficient and curious. Rose doesn't always remember their names; she wonders if she is getting forgetful or something else. Oh well, what the hell, as long as the job gets done who cares. Rose dictates a return letter to Cookie and sends a memo over to Carmen's desk. Carmen will handle the job for her, she is dependable and so much energy too. Rose is worried about the Kenneth Martin with young Captain Winters as master. The ship has now been declared missing and presumed lost. How could a ship over 1300 feet long get lost? The ships GPS signal was still broadcasting but when the location was identified nothing was there. The signal equipment had been placed on the dock, and satellite tracking didn't know the difference. The signal was there but not the ship.

Jones and Braidy are talking about flying over to China to hunt for the missing ship. Braidy,

"Our airplanes would take a long time to fly that far. We would be better off to fly commercial and rent what we need after we get there. Jones asks Carmen,

"Ware in China was our ship supposed to port?"

Carmen tells them the ship was bound for Hong Kong China for a load of containers to be delivered to Los Angeles. The ship had been reporting most of the way, but the last three days nothing. Rose, doesn't even worry any more, she is in charge but sometimes there's nothing she can do about trouble that comes at them from out of the blue. Rose asks,

"Can we ask the local authorities to search for the missing ship? Carmen tells her that she is on it, she has been talking with Chinese police and what's like our Coast Guard but no one knows anything about a 1300-foot-long ship painted in blue over blue. Jones wonders if they have a map of the area in question. Rose doesn't think so, not one that lays on a table or hangs on a wall. She knows there is one in the computer. She isn't the best at computer graphics like using maps, but Joe is our computer whiz.

Joe comes up from his office and he is carrying another bag of those big fat doughnuts from Round the Corner Bakery. The smell gets there ahead of Joe and Jack comes to full attention. He has a nose for pastries that's for sure. Rose and Jones are getting too much padding around their middles and have to say no thanks. Braidy and Carmen and of course Jack don't worry about their figures. Joe opens up a cabinet containing a huge screen located on the wall ware Ken's model rail road and fish tank used to be. The screen gets connected to a computer and maps appear in color on screen. Joe is really good at using computers and Rose like all the rest is fascinated. Joe marks the location of the last good fix on the Kenneth Martin. The GPS signal disappeared, until it was relocated on the dock at Hong Kong China. Joe has a ship shaped icon with the ships name on it. Whenever the icon moves the name travels with it. He has marked the route the ship traveled with dates and times following the lines. The ship isn't anywhere that anyone on seen can identify. Rose isn't getting upset this time, she just can't take this crap any more she says. Jones, lays his hand on her arm and talks softly to her. He will be her rock as always and she does become calmer. Braidy is the curious one, he is wondering how exactly a ship can disappear off the face of the ocean. Braidy,

"how many ways are there for a ship that big or any size to vanish. A ship can sink, can be hijacked, be misdirected by placing the tracking equipment somewhere other than ware the ship is. I vote for the last one, the ship may have been hijacked too, but moving the GPS transmitter will certainly throw us off."

Jones asks Joe,

"joe you're our computer guy, what do you think could have happened to the ship?"

Joe pulling on his lower lip,

"well Mr. Jones, I believe that satellites are providing correct information, and the transmitter on all the ships are reliable, so that leaves us with human intervention."

Jones,

"ok what do you mean exactly?"

Joe sighing,

"unfortunately, Mr. Jones, I have to think that someone on that ship caused signals to change places so to speak. If someone removed all the transmitters from the ship and placed them somewhere else than it would look to us that the ship actually was somewhere else. The signal is coming from the dock. The equipment isn't easy to remove in fact it's nearly impossible. That leads me to another theory, and that is, the transmitters on the ship are turned off or destroyed in place and another transmitter takes over broadcasting the same identification code."

Braidy uses GPS as much as anyone and remarks

"the transmitter on the ship must be similar to the ones on the planes?"

Joe, well the idea is the same, but the actual equipment is much different. I don't know if what I have offered even can be possible, we are throwing around ideas to talk about. Carmen has been flying through various websites on her computer, half listening with one earphone covering her left ear and the right uncovered. She says,

"there are thousands of ships lost mysteriously every year, can that be right? Well anyway there are many reasons including pirates, unexpected storms, mutiny, equipment failures, and that ever famous unknown, It's a mighty big ocean even with ships as large as our container ships. The water is five miles deep or more in many places and if a ship or plane goes down, there is no way to find them. We need to consider that the ship just sank somehow. Rose,

"well ok, but how do we explain the signal on the dock?"

Joe,

"like I said, that transmitter could be another using the tracking information from the ship. If that is the case than its definitely intentional and not accidental. If it is intentional than who and why and what do, they want. It does no one any good if the ship goes to the bottom with everything still aboard Jones,

"who wants to sink a container ship with empty containers on board, the containers have value that's true, but not nearly as much as when they are full.

Rose,

"is it too early for a drink, and do we even have any booze here? Carmen,

"sorry Rose, Jack and I drank it all the last crisis."

Rose,

"no comments from the peanut gallery please."

Carmen says,

"why don't you pick on someone your own size, you're a big bully, you know the last time you said no comment from the peanut gallery, you bought tons and tons of hay for an elephant."

Rose,

"oh yeah, don't remind me of Rosy the elephant."

Jones,

"now girls play nice, after all Jack doesn't complain, right Jack, Jack cuts loose with a big long nasty gaseous stinky fart, and everyone has to move to the other side of the room. Jones, could you please control your dog? Jones,

"so, now he's my dog, when you need him, he is everyone's dog." Jack raids the almost empty doughnut bag and after the last crumbs are down to hatch, he continues to lick the paper.

CHAPTER 57

Cookie is feeling better about his plan, he received a very nice letter from that Rose woman at the shipping company. She tells him he can cook on any ship that needs a good cook. There are cooks retiring often and he should write or call Carmen at company headquarters for more details. Cookie has gotten his appetite back and visits with Mable almost every day. He doesn't think her laugh is so bad any more. She is always glad to see him and leads him to what has become his favorite table. She saves a piece of his favorite pie too, and serves it to him with a flourish. She doesn't ignore other customers not at all, she just makes sure that Cookie gets what he wants first. Finally, Mable works up enough nerve and asks Cookie over for dinner on Sunday when the restaurant is closed in the afternoon. Cookie thinks why not and accepts. He isn't a saint and has needs too like anyone. He does remember to bring flowers for her and she is thrilled. Cookie can walk to her house, the town isn't very large, well not for a man who walks five miles once in a while. Mable has prepared a complete meal in a slow cooker, the roast has been simmering for hours, and the potatoes, carrots onions, are perfect. The meat is so done that he can cut it with a fork and the potatoes are not mushy. Cookie and Mable are enjoying a cup of very good coffee, almost as good as what they had at camp. Cookie doesn't ask her any personal questions; he doesn't want her to ask him any. They talk about the weather, politics, people, sports, fishing, flowers and more. Cookie sits on her couch and she snuggles in beside him. She is warm and everything feels cozy. She is asking if he wants to watch television? Cookie tells her no thanks; this is just fine. He likes listening to quiet once in a while. Mable asks him how that new job is working out? Cookie has forgotten he told her. He has to think for bit, and finally tells her it sucks, he has to work at night. No matter how long you work at night you just never get used to it. Mable has to agree with that.

Mable asks him if he can drive a truck? Cookie, acknowledges he does, why? Mable tells him that her cousin who owns the local cement plant is hiring truck drivers that can handle trucks used to deliver wet cement. The cement trucks take skill to manage, the drums are turning shifting the weight as the truck goes down the road. Cookie tells her he's not interested in driving trucks. He needs to focus on the mission as he now calls it. Besides he is getting to comfortable with Mable, he says he needs to go, and thanks her for dinner. She stops him at her door and smacks him a good one right on the lips. Cookie nearly falls off the step he is so surprised. He stammers his thanks and beats a hasty retreat.

Cookie has ordered the product as he calls it. The explosives will be disguised as special flower used for baking and will be delivered to another town in another name. The mail service is private and uses an actual address. The private mail service rents boxes and if there is something too big for the box than its waiting in a back room to be collected. Cookie is reassured by the company that the stuff will not go off until he wants it to. Cookie orders everything he will need to do the job and decides to visit the court room where the judge presides. The court house has seven court rooms plus the district attorney's offices

Cookie study's everything he can concerning explosives and thinks he knows what he needs to know. After 10 days, he gets a notice that he has some packages to pick up at his secret mail office. Cookie borrows a truck from Mable and drives the 25 miles to collect the big boom stuff. There are detonators too, and he will examine those thoroughly. Cookie goes to court the next day just to watch.

Cookie dresses nice, clean pants and clean shirt, he doesn't wear a tie because he doesn't have one. There are not many others in the court room. Cookie finds a seat near the back. The wooden bench reminds him of a church pew. The Court guy comes in and says,

"all rise for the Honorable Judge Asshole."

Cookie inserts his own name for the judge and it so loud in his head he doesn't hear what is really said. The judge mounts the steps and sits behind the tall desk. He is waring long black robes and has a stack of papers in front of him. He asks,

"how do you plead when the black man is made to stand."

The judge tells the court recorder to enter the plea and says,

"Mr. prosecutor call your first witness."

The first witness is a white woman, she looks oh so delicate hardly having the strength to climb the steps to the witness stand. She is sworn in and sits. The prosecutor is nice to her, gently probing her for testimony. Without prompting she burst into tears, saying she is too upset to continue. Cookie has heard better performances on cartoons. Finally, she resumes and after a few minutes gets it all out. She says that black man right there pointing, stole a large handful of candy from her store. The candy was special and costs a lot. The prosecutor offers his witness to a public defender. The guy is so young, Cookie wonders if he even shaves yet. He tries though and does pretty well. The problem is every question is objected too and the judge says,

"Sustained."

Cookie stays until he can't stand it anymore and simply leaves, and no one notices. The black man gets 10 years in the state penitentiary, and will probably die there if he isn't killed first. Cookie is reminded why this judge has to go, he also knows that the judge happens to own a long white robe and a silk hood.

Cookie writes back to Roses company informing someone named Carmen that he is interested and will arrive in Seattle in two weeks if that would be ok. She sends a letter right away telling him to please come, and that she is looking forward to meeting him. Cookie almost sheds a tear at that one, what a welcome. Cookie brings the materials into work; he has a locker he can lock with a padlock. The material is heavy for its size, it feels like led. Cookie can fire off the explosive remotely and will do so when he is far away. Boy, the technology has improved greatly. Cookie has a ride from a private pilot flying an airplane to Portland Oregon and he can take the train to Seattle from there. The pilot isn't supposed to carry passengers but is willing for $5000 and can keep his mouth shut. Cookie has everything planned out, right down to the minute. He can set off the explosives when he arrives in Portland, he will use a cellphone. Cookie doesn't feel anything about wiping out the judge, prosecutor and anyone else who hates black people just because they have dark skin. Cookie is ready, he has explosives under each desk, and in the court room under the prosecutors table, the judge's bench of course but not under the bench ware common folks may sit. The charges are shaped and will go directly up, right up the judge's slimy ass. That guy will have the worst case of hemorrhoids imaginable. The prosecutors won't' get away either. The entire project takes him a week and he checks it all over each night, he has gotten it right. Cookie is getting excited and can hardly sleep or eat. He doesn't have anything keeping him in Georgia and won't take anything but what he is waring. The times he spends with Mable are the only things he has cared about for a long while now.

The big day comes for Cookie and he simply walks out of his room shutting the door but not bothering to lock. There is nothing he has left behind to identify him, and even if people remember him, they don't know his name. He has wiped the computer clean removing the hard drive and smashing it with a sledge hammer. The remains he takes to the river after placing it in wet cement. The cement looks like a rock and will rest on the bottom under 30 feet of water. As far as Cookie knows no one knows that he ever existed except for Mable and even she doesn't know him as anything different than Cookie.

Cookie walks to the little airport ware he meets the pilot who flies them to Portland. The guy is short and scrawny. He chews gum constantly and pops it. Cookie doesn't care, he just climbs in and puts on his seatbelt, he has ear buds and a small player. He has sawmill sounds recorded on the memory stick. He misses the boys from the mill and likes hearing sounds that reminds him of better times. The pilot is a bit rusty, Cookie thinks, the takeoff roll wasn't very clean. They get up in the air and are flying mostly west. The plane is a Beech Craft Barren and is comfortable. They fly along not saying much, theirs the drone of the engine and the smacking of the pilot's gum. Cookie would rather just hear the engine than the gum, but oh well.

After several fuels stops and bathroom breaks, they arrive in Portland Oregon. Cookie pays the man, the last of his life's savings and finds his way to a city bus. He will stay in a Hostel for this night and take a train tomorrow Cookie is hungry for the first time in a long while and decides to find a little café like Mable's. After he orders, he looks around and decides it's not the same. Cookie sighs and finishes coffee, boy that's not the same either. Cookie walks to the nearby Hostel and finds his bed, the bed costs him $60 a night and seems like highway robbery. Oh well one night is ok he supposes. In the morning, it is raining lightly and Cookie finds a nearest bus stop, and after two hours gets to the train station. The train for Seattle will leave in 20 minutes and he buys a one-way ticket. He has planned this so well; he stands out in the rain and makes the call. There is nothing to confirm if the signal went through or not, it has to be an act of faith. After cookie makes the call of all calls, he drops the phone down a storm sewer after removing the battery and Sim card. The card he breaks up into tiny pieces and swallows them. The peace's will come out sooner or later and down the hole they will go. Cookie boards the train finds a seat and falls asleep. He sleeps away while the court house in no-wares Ville Georgia blows sky high. The explosives are more powerful than Cookie planned. Not only will Judge KKK never have hemorrhoids again as a matter of fact he doesn't even have an asshole or a chair to sit it on. The prosecutor's office is completely gone, the entire end of the building went into orbit, and some of the parts may still be up there. Cookie isn't even worried, he sleeps almost all the way to Seattle, waking up just in Time to stagger off the train. It's raining in Seattle too, it must rain every ware in this part of the country Cookie calls Roses company and talks to someone named Carmen,

"hello Ms. Carmen, this is Cookie, and I am here now in Seattle."

"ok good, Mr. Jones and Mr. Braidy will come and get you, they want to see you."

Cookie has to think about that, now who are Jones and Braidy again? Then he remembers, those guys were the men who rescued that black guy, John-John was it? Cookie tells Carmen ware he will be waiting and gets some coffee for himself while he waits.

CHAPTER 58

Rose asks Joe if he will fly to Hong Kong China to quietly investigate the missing ship. They have gotten nowhere with the Chinese authorities. They don't have any idea what happened to the ship and can't be bothered to look any more. Rose has provided Joe with contacts the company uses to generate new business and to satisfy older customers. The contacts go way back to her father's days in Hong Kong. She doesn't even know if all the people are still working or alive for that matter

Joe takes a lap top computer loaded down with files names and contacts he will need. He has also loaded in software that may help him to track down the ship. He doesn't want to miss anything; it may be possible that the ship has been painted another color. That would be a big job but for a billion dollar plus ship it could be worth it. Joe travels light taking a minimum of clothing and papers. Most of everything he will need is in the computer on a smart phone or he can get it there. Joe is driven to the airport by Rose, and Joni rides along. She has gotten closer to him and says she will miss him and please be careful Rose tells him that too, Joe feels like a kid going off to college. Rose wraps him in a big hug, and Joni kisses him soundly. He hugs back and waves them good bye. Joe catches a flight directly to Hong Kong that is better, and decides to study his computer while traveling. Joe flies first class, Rose insisted on that, and when he gets settled in, he promptly falls asleep.

Jones and Braidy meet Cookie at the Train station and recognize him right away. He looks thinner, and a little grayer but it's the same hero they remember. Jones and Braidy shake his hand warmly, and invite him to the waiting van. cookie is quiet, he isn't so certain about all this memory business. He wants to keep a low profile. Jones,

"so, Cookie how you been, and are you hungry?"

"well I'm ok and I am a little hungry.'"

Braidy likes that idea, and ask,

"gentlemen, what's your pleasure?"

Cookie doesn't have any idea, he just wants a small café, if there is any. Braidy and Jones know of one and say he will like this place. Its Italian, but they can fix anything you like. The bread is heavenly and the place is family owned. They go to the downstairs Italian café close to the company headquarters building and Cookie finds they are right, it is nice. Cookie eats more than he is used to and Braidy says he admires a good appetite. Jones orders a Sheff salad and gobbles down too much fresh bread. Man, oh man is that stuff ever good.

The three men go to headquarters building and up to the office in the private elevator. When Cookie steps in the office he meets Jack. Cookie has forgotten how big that dog is, and says,

"hey big boy, remember me?"

Of course, Cookie doesn't expect a dog to remember him but Jack barks once and sits back holding up his paw. Cookie is surprised at that and stoops down to accept the offer. Cookie looks over at Jones, wondering if the dog remembers him? Jones nods, and says,

"Jack is a smart dog; he knows more and more every day I think."

Jack doesn't deny it, and wolfs softly.

Rose comes bustling in smelling sweet like roses, she has been above playing in her roses again. She comes right over to Cookie holding out her small hands,

"I'll bet your Cookie from Georgia?"

Cookie can't deny that, and tells her yes mam. Rose takes both of is rough tough old hands in both of hers and says

"we're so glad you could join us; we are so very proud of our long-time workers."

A pretty young Spanish girl comes over from behind a desk by the windows. She introduces herself as Carmen and shakes his hand like rose did. Cookie almost sheds a tear; he has never had such a welcome before.

Rose tells him that he can use one of the empty apartments if he likes until the Prince Albert sails in three days. The Albert is a; large tug boat and has been repainted in the new blue over darker blue colors. The ship is 250 feet long and is tough and has an excellent galley on her. Jones remembers the Prince Albert when he sailed on her long ago now.

Rose asks him if he is hungry? Cookie oh no, these boys fed me well at a little Italian café around the corner. Rose admits that is a nice place and they have such wonderful bread.

CHAPTER 59

Cookie is directed to a two-bedroom apartment three floors below and Carmen asks him if he needs anything? Cookie wants to ask her something but is bashful,
 "excuse me mam, I don't mean to pry, but are you blind?'
 Carmen lays her small hand on his old shoulder and says yes, she is, and I bet I fooled you, didn't I?
 Cookie tells her that his old Grandmother was blind and he always helped her go to church, and he has never forgotten. Carmen says,
 "Would you like to sit and visit with me for a while?"
 Cookie has been lonely for so long for youngsters that he gulps back a tear and says
 "yes, thank you, just for a little while if you don't mind."
 Carmen invites him into her apartment, it is nice, she has decorated just the way she likes. The furniture is mostly wicker and squeaks when they sit on it. Carmen has the news on quietly on a television in the corner. She doesn't really care what's on, she likes the quiet murmur. Cookie sees the screen just in time to see the court house go up in a fireball that rises 100 feet in the air. The fire is so hot that fire crews can't even get near the building. The news caster says that the building is only a hole in the ground, nothing is left. Cookie is shocked, he guesses he over did it. Carmen is asking,
 "Cookie, are you alright?"
 Oh yes, he answers, I'm just watching something on the news. She wonders what it is, and turns up the sound.
 The news reporter states that fire authorities have no idea why the 75-year-old building blew up. Arsan is suspected, there are no

survivors police believe that 11 prosecutors were at their desks when the explosion occurred. The court rooms were mostly empty except for Judge Gil Terrance. The Judge resided with his wife and two dogs in Atlanta. He was known as the hanging judge. He never sentenced anyone to less than the full sentence allowed by law. Cookie nearly weeps with joy, at last those bastards get what they deserved.

Carmen is getting worried; she has been calling his name with no response. Finally, he answers, saying excuse me Ms. Carmen, I use to live in that little town where the court house blew up today, or was it yesterday. Carmen tells him it doesn't matter, it was recently.

Cookie comes back to himself and tells Carmen he needs to get some rest and tells her good night and thank you. Carmen walks him to his door and says if he needs anything to knock on her door, she will hear, she sleeps lightly.

Cookie sees his new home for the first time, it's a beautiful ship painted in blue over blue. It looks powerful and could move the world if it wanted to. He finds his way around the galley noting that the freezer is fully stocked and so is the pantry. The oven is quality and there are enough pieces of cooking equipment he can cook anything. He will really enjoy this job. The ship sails off in the morning and Cookie feels a sense of relief, no one can possibly know where he is gotten to. Cookie meets the crew and he can tell they like him right away. They all call him Cookie before he even tells them his name. The captain is a funny guy, with an Irish brogue. The ship will be towing oil platforms around and moving ships that are disabled. Cookie doesn't care what this ship does, he is more interested in the fellows who sail on her.

CHAPTER 60

In Atlanta, there is a big funeral for the judge, only in Spirit, the judge's body can't be found. The judge, prosecutor, clerks and a few other nasty folks are flying in outer space. The blast was heard for 10 miles and made the earth shake. Cookie really may have over done it, but still if you're going to do the job do it right. Cookie reads about the big funeral over the news on someone's computer and shakes his head with all the rest. Only he knows what happened and that's the way it will stay. He will go to is grave with the secret. Still sometimes he wonders how Mable is doing, she was so nice to an old man. Oh well, life goes on and he really applies himself, cooking some of his best dishes for his new boys

The Prince Albert sails out to South America to a place near Venezuela. Cookie doesn't even know what kind of place this is. He has never sailed before; he is worried about getting sea sick but the ships bumping up and down doesn't bother him at all. He likes it, it puts him to sleep at night kind of like being rocked in a cradle. Cookie is happy in his world and even starts to sing a little tune from his childhood. He isn't loud but loud enough for guys to listen. They tell him that's really good, sing louder man. Cookie looks around in surprise and is embarrassed.

"What are you bums doing loafing around here, don't you got no work to do?"

"We just want to hear you sing Cookie."

Cookie is feeling expansive and says, "Oh hell, come on in and shut that door."

Cookie is pulling out a cookie sheet of hot chocolate chip cookies that drive most normal diners wild with desire. He brings out a gallon of milk and passes around glasses and piles of still warm cookies. The men gather around and with their mouths full drinking and chewing ask him to pleas sing for them.

Cookie says, "Alright I warned you, now you're going to get it!"

Cookie has a fine tenor voice and he sings Oh Danny Boy and My Wild Irish Rose for them. Just then the Dorr is flung open and theirs the captain looking around in surprise. He doesn't say a word, instead helps himself to the cookies and one of the guys offers him a glass of milk. Cookie doesn't know what to do, he hardly knows this captain. He is beginning to turn red.

Captain Murphy says, "please man don't stop, after all I'm your captain and I order you to sing like a bird."

"Ok captain, but I warned you like the others here."

Cookie gets into it then and really belts out the tunes, he sees one sailor dash off and, in a minute, he is back with a squeeze box. Another grabs a cookie for the road and goes off for a guitar. Theirs another and another and soon there are instruments all over the galley. Cookie sings his heart out finally breaking down and just plain sobbing with pure joy. He had no idea that any of his boys cared anything about his old music. The captain is smiling big time. Finally, one fellow asks,

"say captain, who's driving the boat?"

"oh, someone is don't worry, maybe we better check just to be sure. The guy nearest the door says he will go and grabs up a hand full of freshly baked cookies. Captain,

"you make sure some of those cookies make it to the bridge now."

Not all cruises on the Prince Albert are so Mary, things can get tough when seas are tossing them around like they were a cork. Captain thanks Cookie and the others do to and back to work for all of them. Cookie is happy for the first time in a long time. He can't stop singing and decides to start something good for supper

CHAPTER 61

Rose is getting concerned, they haven't heard from Joe for days. He called them on his satellite phone when he first arrived in Hong Kong but not since. Jones ask Nancy to try and track his phones signal but she gets nothing. Jones, keeps quiet, he has a very bad feeling about Joe. First the ship than the man, what's going on. Joni is beside herself with anxiety she misses Joe more than she wants to say. Carmen goes to her and tells her she is willing to listen if she wants to talk. Joni knows that Carmen and Joe once were dating but Carmen assures her that that's in the past. Joni and Carmen decide to go out for dinner and walk to the little downstairs Italian café. Joni is ok now; she and Don came here on their first date and the place had some memories. She thinks the food is more important than old memories and offers to help Carmen with the steps. Carmen just swats Joni on the but with her cane and says,

"move that big ass out of my way woman, your holding up progress."

Joni goes down the steps ahead of her and smiles at her mighty friend. How far this young girl has come in such a short time. The two women are welcome this time by the owner, he explains that his beautiful daughter is also his smart one is going to the university. They can hear how proud he is he tells them that it's just Mamma and him now, like in the beginning. His wife comes out of the kitchen with a heaping basket of hot rolls straight from the oven. The butter is soft and spreads over the hot bread like it belong there.

Jones and Rose are visiting the greenhouse on the top of the building and are talking about Joe and the missing ship. Jack is in a corner, on a fluffy dog bed, blue over dark blue of course in color. He is snoring lightly dreaming of chasing rabbits back home on the farm Jones thinks. His paw scratches are like he is running and he lets out a muffled wolf. Rose has come to love that Jack as much as Jones and enjoys long walks with him in the park and on the beech too. Rose,

Jones, have I told you how much I love you?

Jones says just every day about twice an hour but keep it up I don't mind. Rose shrugs and says,

"well I just wanted to be sure, don't you know."

They have a small grill in the doorway of the greenhouse and rose is making some of Jones's favorites Polish Sausages. She gets them from an Italian meat market and they are oh so good, she puts them into freshly made rolls from the Round the Corner Bakery. The Polish Sausage and the fresh rolls along with a good cold beer and they are contented. Rose has won some prizes for her roses; she grows very special roses that are rare and difficult to grow. Jones thinks it's because she talks to them often. Braidy thinks it's all of Jack's product that does the trick, it's not true she doesn't make Jack make deposits in her rose beds.

CHAPTER 62

Barbra fishes every day; she boards mostly men at the dock and guides them out to a likely spot. Sometimes there are women, usually much younger than the men they are with. She keeps quiet not saying a word, if those guys want younger women who are probably not their wives its none of her business. If they pay her and add a tip than she is ok with anything. She is jolly and gets everyone to smile and laugh at her good-natured humor. Today's gathering includes two very young women who aren't properly dress that's for sure. They are waring very short shorts and hardly enough top to cover their nipples. Barbra likes to dress casual waring cargo shorts and shirts with the name of her company a crossed the front, and sometimes she doesn't even ware shoes. Barbra goes about her business with ease untangling lines, baiting hooks and helping the fat guys pull in their catches. She does it in such a way that they think they are doing all the work; she is always fun and helpful. When the fish is finally aboard, she praises the fisherman like he has just caught a wale not a 20-pound fish. Barbra doesn't forget her village friends and always brings them fish that the fishermen don't want to keep or some she catches herself.

There are two men and two women, the good news is, the women don't want to fish, only the guys. Barbra is always glad not to have to do more work. The women want to be looked at and don't like fishing at all. The men think that if they catch big fish their girlfriends will be really impressed, but mostly they are bored. Barbra knows all of that but keeps still and does her job. Barbra has a new radio installed in her boat; it is one that Braidy has gotten for her. Braidy installed it for her and showed her how to use it. She is idling along with the two lines dragging off the back of the boat when she heir's,

"Mayday, Mayday, can anyone hear me?" "this is The Blue Sea calling, May Day May Day, can anyone hear me over."

Barbra doesn't know what to do, she gets nervous and thinks what does that mean. Finally, after no one else answers she picks up the mike and answers,

"Hello May Day, this is Barbra, do you need help?"

"Hello Barbra, this is John, we need help please, our boat is sinking fast, theirs water coming over the main deck."

"ok John, where are you?"

"I don't know exactly, we left Seattle this morning before light and have headed mostly west.

"do you have a GPS?"

"no afraid not, we didn't think we would ever need one."

Barbra has a friend in the coast guards and tries to remember how to call them, finally she does. She says to John,

"do you have a life boat or life jackets?"

"yes, we have life jackets and have them on."

Barbra settles down and speaks more clearly. She directs them,

"ok John, first of all how many are there, and can you see any land around you?"

"ok, yes there are three of us, and there is no land near us."

"ok John, stay calm and sit tight, I'm calling for help, can you continue to talk on your radio?"

"well only until the boat goes under."

Barbra tells him to hold on, she'll just get right back to him. She calls her Coast guard friend informing him of the emergency. The Coast Guard want more information, she hasn't any. She says she can try to get a better idea of the direction of the radio signal. She asks,

"can you hear John's call?"

"no sorry Barbra, we're getting nothing."

She tells him that she must be fairly close, and will try to get closer to John's position

John and Kathy and their 10-year-old daughter are inches from sinking, the boat is a single massed sail boat 35 feet long and is a well-used craft. John hired a company to check over the boat, and trusted their judgement, and now the boat is sinking. John sells real-estate and isn't much with mechanical devices and is terrified. He stays aboard as long as he can, talking to Barbra, but soon every part of the boat will be under. The water is inching its way to the top of the stand that holds the electronics including the radio. John,

"hello Barbra, I can't talk much longer, the water is about to drown out the radio. Can you help us?"

Barbra has been moving the antenna in differing direction and has decided that John's boat is to the south-west and heads that way. She tells John to keep his family together, and don't move any more than necessary. John,

"what, why, do you mean there are sharks?"

Barbra,

"just do as I say, you'll be ok, and to herself says, I hope."

The guys are indignant that their fishing will be interrupted and complain to her. She isn't the same silly goofy island girl any longer, she says to the boys,

"this is a matter of life and death, now sit down and shut up or I will feed you to the sharks."

They are shocked and simply do as they are told. Barbra knows that she has to try and help, it's the law of the sea. After all she could be in trouble herself someday. She drives her boat in the direction she thinks is the right one and scans the ocean for anything. The women are more helpful than the men and offer to help her. She tells them to help her look for three people floating in the water waring orange life jackets, John told her the color. She drives her boat fast, the new Diesel engine is roaring away, with 50 more horse power than the last one. The engine is new costing her more than she could afford, allowing Braidy to loan her the money. She sure loves her man, and is thinking about him now. She is wondering if he could fly over and help her look. The Coast Guard said they were on their way to her location and will be here long before Braidy can. She brings out a pair of binoculars that she got from her father and looks forward and all around. She see's nothing, just looking. One of the young women sees what she is doing and ask, "excuse me mam, but I could climb up on top of the cabin and look from there. Maybe I can see further higher up."

Barbra looks at her and sees she is sincere and says yes thank you good. The girls name is Elli finally Barbra remembers, and says,

"good Elli, that will help I think."

Elli looks at Barbra's jacket that is hanging on a hook, with a question, and Barbra nods yes.

Barbra is getting desperate trying to find John and his family but nothing. She wonders if she has gone past them and slows the boat, the waves have been slapping against the bough and now the ride is easier. The men decide to come out from the cabin, decide to get in on the action. Barbra is still mad at these guys and commands them help look for John. They are submissive and obey, shading their eyes with their hands. The day isn't bright and for an instant she wonders why. Elli shouts out from the top of the cabin roof, and is pointing to the left. Barbra looks to her left and feels sick. She sees nothing but bloody remains, the sharks have been feeding on John and his family. Barbra didn't know any of them, but she sheds tears thinking about those pore people. She especially feels bad for the little girl Barbra knows of this part of the ocean and doesn't bring charters near. The sharks often feed here and will devour anything or anyone. She has seen some sharks that are 18 feet long with mouths full of row after row of teeth. Barbra circles around the seen, the guys turn green and one loses his breakfast over the side. The women let out screams and hide their faces not wanting to see anymore. Barbra stops the boat and probes in the water amongst the debris, she finds three shredded life jackets and lots of blood. The people are all gone and the boat is completely under. She calls the Coast Guard telling them of what she finds or hasn't found. The Guardsman who answers is sympathetic and says he's sorry. Barbra,

"do you need me to stay here?"

"yes, until we get there, the cutters are ten minutes away from your position, thank goodness for your GPS. Barbra drops the anchor and asks,

"are you guys alright?"

Everyone isn't alright but say they are. She decides it may be time for a spot of Rum and offers the bottle all around. The women drink right out of the bottle, and the men shake their heads no. Barbra thinks to herself well it looks like the women are the tough ones.

The coast Guard cutter arrives right on time; the GPS makes estimates more accurate. She invites a lieutenant to her boat and he notices the Rum bottle and she offers. He says no thanks not now but maybe later? Barbra knows he's on duty and tells him anytime. The fishermen have gone back into the cabin and the women are as far from the blood seen as the boat will allow. The Guards says there's nothing to save here, there's no body parts they can grabbed. He wants to know if she got anyone's names, and the name of the boat? She tells him the name ok, and John's name too, that's all she has. He tells her its ok, she did good, he will find out what he needs to know from the registration of the boat.

CHAPTER 63

Barbra delivers the four back to the dock and decides to try and call the Braidy fellow. Mac tells her that Braidy is just now landing, he can give him a message. She says,
"oh well no thanks Mr. Mac, I'll be coming over there soon, just keep him there until I am there too. Barbra has a small motor cycle for getting around with when she is ashore and roars off to the hanger. The hanger takes a while to get to, and Braidy will wait for her she knows
    Braidy flies in with one of the King Air's and the plane lands itself he thinks. He has done this so many times that the movements are automatic. He knows he will have to constantly remind himself to stay awake. He taxi's over to the hanger and Mac and the guys take over. They fill it with fuel and wash it clean. They take good care of all the aircraft but especially the King Air's. Braidy looks around for Barbra and doesn't see her. He asks the guys if there's any coffee left? Mac waves him into the hanger ware theirs always hot coffee. Braidy has been feeling extra tired lately and needs to coffee up to be awake. He sits back in Mac's office chair placing his big feet on the desk. He leans back in Mac's chair and jumps up in a start. The chair is missing a wheel and the wheel's arm has slipped off the wood block it was on. Braidy nearly falls over backwards, he saves himself barely but gets a coffee bath all down his front. Braidy pulls out his little note book he always carry's and writes in big letters, Chair for Mac, urgent.
    Finally, he hears Barbra's little motor cycle buzzing up the drive and gets up to meet her. Barbra,

"well Mr. Braidy, I see your having trouble finding that very pretty mouth, you got more on the outside than the inside I'll bet, do you need a mother?"

Braidy swats her rather soundly on her very nice but and pulls her into a bear hug. She says,

"pleas Mr. Braidy sir, I can't hardly breathe."

Braidy lifts her little motor cycle up into the back of his truck and invites her to come with him. She looks at him and the truck with her transportation on board and says,

"I think I will, since you've captured my bike."

Barbra tells Braidy all about her morning and he listens not saying anything until she is finished. Braidy knows that there are many people every year who are lost in the ocean, and some are without any apparent reason. He fixes simple food for them to eat and they turn on the TV to watch an old movie. The movie is one they have never seen, it doesn't matter, they both fall asleep snuggling on the couch.

CHAPTER 64

Joni is missing Joe so much it hurts. She is constantly asking Rose and Carmen if they have heard anything, and what are they going to do about Joe. Rose hears her frustration and pain and has been thinking a great deal of the problem She doesn't want to send anyone else over there, she is afraid something bad will happen to them too. Rose gathers her people together and is asking them what they think. Nancy says, she can go, after all her job is security and she is responsible. Rose shakes her head no, not your fault. There's something about the missing ship and the missing man that really stinks. Jones agrees with her, and looks at Braidy. He and Braidy have been through many scrapes together now, Jones knows he can depend on his friend. Braidy isn't experienced in combat but he knows a world of other resources. Rose sees what her two favorite men are hatching and says a very adamant NO! The two guys shrug and say they will come up with another idea. Nancy tells them that she can look for a private detective type they can hire to do the job. Jones,

"do you mean like Colombo?"

Rose looks at him like she doesn't know him and Jones, admits that may have been only a Midwest thing. Braidy keeps quiet, he remembers Colombo very well. Nancy asks Carmen if she can research private detectives on the internet. She goes to work, with one earphone off so she can still hear what's being discussed. She has made the speech so fast on her computer that to Jones the sound is like an auctioneer.

. The speech is so fast he cannot make out a single word but Carmen has gotten used to it and knows it all. Jones is so proud of

Carmen he has to feel good about her, he hasn't had a lot of successes in his life but watching Carmen helps him to forget the mistakes

Rose likes Nancy's idea the best, hiring a private detective means that no one from her company has to take chances. After all they are executives not hired gun fighters. The detective company is trained in hunting and dealing with criminals, they are not. Nancy brings rose the lap top she has been looking at and shows her the information. Rose doesn't know anything about detective agencies and says so. Nancy tells her that she wants to bring someone in for an interview. Rose asks Carmen when she has time and Carmen pulls up yet another program. She has Roses calendar endear and tells her that next Tuesday looks good in the morning. Rose says isn't that the time I spend with my roses? Carmen answers yes, but this is necessary? Rose says My rose time is necessary too, and why is my rose time always first to go? Carmen says sorry about that.

CHAPTER 65

Joe doesn't know where he is, he was grabbed just outside the international airport in Hong Kong and shoved into the back of a waiting car. He is a strong guy but when there are four bigger stronger determined bad guys there's not much, he can do. The men are organized and knew he was coming. Joe doesn't know Hong Kong well and soon was lost with all the turns. He is surprised they haven't placed a blind fold over his eyes. He believes that's a bad thing for him, they will probably kill him. Joe doesn't give up; he's always looking for his chance. It's really difficult sitting between these two huge Chinese fellows. The car smells like Chinese takeout and old sweat He tries to keep track of how far they have traveled at least but loses track of time. They bring him to a large building with a door big enough to drive in with a truck. The floor is open with only one other vehicle, a beat-up old truck. Joe is pushed out the open door after the big guy on his left gets out. He is taken into an office toward the back of the building. There is a man with the biggest head Joe has ever seen on a human. The head is enormous and is square. The man blinks constantly and sniffles often. He has a winy voice but speaks passable English. He tells Joe to sit down, and one of the bad guys shoves him down on a metal folding chair. Joe is out muscled that's for sure, and just agrees with everything that anyone says. The man wines out,

"you are Joe Blow? Joe is taken by surprise than remembers oh yes that's what he told the big guys at the airport when they grabbed him. Joe listens with his ears but keeps his eyes on the square head's desk. The guy is asking Joe if he is in charge of shipping in the Big Lift Shipping and Logging company. Joe doesn't know what he is asking and says so. Square Head,

"You contact Mr. Chang with China electric?".

Joe does recall that he did, and says yes. Mr. Square Head brings out a small stack of papers and lays them in front of Joe. Joe recalls the contract and nods.

"you are Joe, but your name isn't Blow."

Joe smiles some, finding some amusement with that little bit of resistance. Joe finally gets enough of this weird character and demands,

"so, what in hell is this all about and where is our ship?"

Mr. Square Head waves his muscle back, making calming motions with his puffy hand. The men behind lower their weapons. Joe, well why does my name matter, what do you want. And why steel a ship that's empty. Square Head moves the papers back towards his side of the desk. He neatens them up by tapping the edges on the top of his desk. Joe has no idea what's going on here and tells him that

Square Head brings out another stack of papers, and shows them to Joe. The document is in Chinese and he can't read them. Joe,

"excuse me, whatever your name is, I don't read Chinese."

For some reason, Square Head takes off in a painful hi-pitched laugh that hurts Joe's ears and that gets the goons going too. Joe turns red and says,

"I don't suppose you can translate this for me?"

Square Head, tells Joe that it is standard contract retaining the services of a Chinese owned container ship, and the ship is the same size as their missing ship. Joe, looks up at that, and wants to know more.

Square Head tells Joe that their ship is missing too, and they thought that Big Lift Shipping and Lumbers must have stolen it. Joe begins to understand and says,

"listen, let's try and be civilized here, we both have a missing ship and they are the same size you say? Square Head

"we believe your company stole our ship, because you are that greedy."

Joe, may I ask your name?

Mr. Square Head says his name is Chung, that will do for now. Joe continues, ok can we compare what we both have lost, I can show you everything if someone could bring me my laptop computer. Mr. Chong nods to one of the big guys and he brings Joe's computer. Joe is looking around for a place to plug it in, he sees none. Mr. Chong shrugs and gets up; he invites Joe to follow him to some stairs and they climb to the upper level. There are living quarters above like this in so many buildings in China. The outlet is for 220 volts but that's alright, Joe has an adapter. Joe plugs it in and after a few seconds the screen comes up. Joe types in his password and files appear like magic on the screen. Joe invites Mr. Chong closer and uses the curser to trace the route traveled by the Kenneth Martin. The ship travels at 25 knots and the progress is clear on the map. When the ship nears Hong Kong the ships image disappears for an instant, Joe hadn't noticed that before, he wonders why. Joe studied the map thoroughly before leaving Seattle. Oh well, Joe tells Mr. Chong,

"we followed our ship to here, pointing out the spot, there was a blink, then the tracking resumes over here pointing to the place where the ship returned to its original route."

Mr. Chong is following and brings out his own lap top computer. He has a similar map showing a similar track shortly after the Kenneth Martins track. Joe compares the two tracks noticing that the two ships could be one ship they are that close. Joe says to Mr. Chong,

"if you allow me to call home to let them know I'm alright I promise you I will stay here until we get this problem resolved. Mr. Chong agrees and offers Joe a satellite phone. Joe notes that Mr. Chung's phone is identical to the ones they all use. Joe dials the headquarters building and Joni answers,

"big Lift Shipping and logging company."

Joe answers,

"this is Big Lift Joe calling the pretties girl in all of Seattle, how are you?"

Joni faints dead away, she just falls onto her face on her desk. Gerry was coming by with a big load of today's mail and stops to stair. He knows Miss Joni isn't feeling good and calls for help. He has a button that Rose has given him to be used only if there's an emergency. The security come running from everywhere it seems and with their guns drawn see Joni laying a crossed her desk. Gerry is terrified and settles to the floor with his hands over his head.

Joe returns to Mr. Chong asking about the ships and the cargo. Joe asks him what about the similarities?

"yes, they are similar, and they were both assigned the same cargo, and now no one carries the electronics to your Los Angeles."

Joe is asking, what color is your ship? Mr. Chong looks at Joe,

"what difference does the color make?"

Joe tells him that their ships colors used to be red and white and they are blue over darker blue. Joe is wondering if somehow Ken's past is haunting them still. Chong tells Joe that their ships are black with white lettering.

Joe feeling calmer after the conversation, He asks

"why did you have to kidnap me, we will cooperate of course, all you have to do is ask."

Mr. Chong doesn't answer instead offers Joe refreshments and Joe thinks that's a good sign if he knows something about these people.

In headquarters building, medical people rush to Joni, soon she rises up and picks up the phone, there's no one there. She is beginning to wonder is she imagined the call. She plays back the recording that occurs with all calls and there is Joe's voice asking her how she is. Joni calls up to the office and tells Carmen that she has heard from Joe, and she has a number to call him back with. The security dismisses the EMT's and they help Gerry up from the floor. He is excited over Ms. Joni and gives her a hug. Joni hugs him back just being so glad to have heard from Joe at last. Joni uses her key card to take the elevator to the top floor and is ushered into the office. Carmen and Rose are excited to hear about Joe too and want to know all the details. Rose gets the number from the caller ID and tries calling. She hears only Chinese and doesn't understand a word

Joe asks Mr. Chong if he may use the phone again and this time calls Roses direct line. Rose nearly drops her phone when Joe calls her. She doesn't faint but Joni is jumping up and down wanting to talk to him. Rose, asks,

"joe, are you alright?"

Joe tells her he is ok, and is working on the problem he will let her know when he knows. Rose says,

"say Joe could you talk to Joni for a minute?

Rose and the others move away to allow Joni to have a little privacy. Joni gets more information as Joe can tell her, and she will tell everyone else. Rose is so relieved she does a little dance around with Joni. Jack just looks bored not interested in dancing

Joe and Mr. Chong come to a better understanding concerning their missing ships, they are both honest men and that helps when dealing with missing ships.

CHAPTER 66

In Georgia police are considering the court house explosion to be arson There are 10 detectives investigating the crime, they come from Atlanta and some from the state too. They question everyone for miles around and get nowhere. No one knows anything about the bombing or whatever it was. When they try, and talk with black folks they get nothing but, yes sir, no sir, I sure don't know nothing. The county is a mess, many cases are on the dockets for hearings and trial but nowhere to hold courts. The prosecutors are brought in from the Attorney General's office to fill in, but with the prosecutors went the records too. No one knows anything about most cases and everything gets put on hold. The substitute prosecutors don't want the evidence offered by the defense lawyers, after all they could have changed everything in their favor. The district has to bring in judges from other districts to fill in. The judges can hear cases however the chain of evidence has been broken they say. They will have to release many prisoners because of lack of evidence. The attorney general doesn't like that at all and tells everyone to place a hold on all cases and no one gets out of jail.

Cookie is happier than he has ever been, he cooks for his boys plays music and is accepted by the entire crew. He reads news on computers from time to time and catches the headline from the town he used to live in. He reads about the legal system being disrupted to the point that they may have to consider releasing prisoners. The news is nice to hear but Cookie knows that it will never happen. The corruption is so deep there that nothing will ever change. One of the guy's notices Cookie reading the news and asks,

"hey Cookie, you alright?"

Cookie tells him oh yeah, I'm kind of interested in legal things, and noticed the headlines."

The sailor tells Cookie that the place he's reading about is 5000 miles away and it can't have anything to do with them. Cookie slaps his friend on the back and says,

"you know you're right, let's see if there are any cookies left?"

CHAPTER 67

Joe and Mr. Chung are sipping tea and tasting little cakes his wife brings out for them. Joe thinks Mr. Chung isn't so bad after all, he is worried about his ship, and is just as confused as Joe. Mr. Chung's wife is a tiny woman not over 5 feet tall and weighing less than Carmen back home. She is efficient and moves in and out of the room bringing refreshment seemingly all on her own. She doesn't say anything and her looks are quick darting back and forth between Joe and Mr. Chung. The conversation touches on companies and management. The company that Mr. Chung manages and owns isn't nearly as large as Joe's company. Mr. Chung indicates that they have 4 ships and loosing even 1 ship is disastrous. Joe tells him that he and his people will find out what happened to their ships. Joe wants to ask Rose if they should use another ship to transport the cargo. Joe isn't sure what to do about Mr. Chong's interest. Why would a manufacturer request two ships for the same cargo? Joe asks,

"Mr. Chung, do you know if there are two shipments to be moved or only the one?"

"as far as we know there's only one cargo, we received the new order a few days ago, when did you receive yours?"

Joe tells him they got their orders over a month ago, now, and maybe we need to talk with the manufacturer.

Mr. Chung agrees with him and says that he can contact them. Joe asks to barrow the phone again, and Mr. Chung waves one of his big guys over and says,

"please bring Mr. Joe's phone to him?"

The young man has been standing in the doorway out of sight but near enough to respond to a call for help. Mr. Chung tells Joe that the men are all his sons. Joe looks after his tiny wife and wonders how! Mr. Chung sees his look and says,

"Chinese women are incredible don't you think?" Joe just nods.

Chong's son brings Joe his satellite phone and he speed dials the company number,

"hello, oh hi Carmen, everything is ok here, we still have a missing ship but at least no one wants to beat me up any more."

Carmen tells him that's good, she doesn't want to have to come all the way over there and have to defend Joe. She asks him how can she help? Joe gives her the information that he and Chung have been discussing. Carmen says she will fill Rose in and is he using his own phone now? Joe says he is, Mr. Chung returned it to him, it looks like Mr. Chung also has a missing ship, and his company was ordered to carry the same cargo as their ship. Rose is listening in on Carmen's phone, she has turned on the speaker so that others can hear too. Rose asks,

"what do you want to do now? Joe tells her about talking with the manufacturer with Mr. Chung to try and get to the bottom of that little mystery Rose asks him,

"Joe, do you need anything, can we send anything or should someone else come there?"

Joe tells her no, he's good for now, let's find out more information and then talk about what to do. Rose says ok, but be sure and stay in touch. Rose steps back and Jones asks,

"are you able to send us the name of Mr. Chung's shipping company, does he mind?"

Chung has been listening and nods in agreement, he will cooperate in any way he can, just ask

Joe and Chung visit the manufacturer asking about the shipping order mix up. The management is evasive, not committing themselves to any answer. They have no cargo to be shipped to anywhere in America presently. The company has shipped many times before with Joe's company but not now no need, thank you very much.

Mr. Chung and Joe are both unhappy to hear that one, they decide to have lunch, and Mr. Chung and Joe are driven to Mr. Chong's favorite Italian restaurant. Joe asks, "so, Mr. Chung I thought you would want a Chinese restaurant. Mr. Chung,

"oh, no I hate Chinese restaurant, I've had everything before, I like Italian because it's so different than fish and rice."

Joe,

"well I understand I think."

CHAPTER 68

Joe and Mr. Chung decide they can't do much more currently, they will need more help than they have. Joe provides Mr. Chung with all the information he has concerning the ship, its crew and Captain Winters, and Joe will contact him often to stay updated. They agreed to hire a local detective agency to look for missing ships and crew. Mr. Chung is worried about his missing ship and hopes his company can survive. Loosing 25 per cent of a company's revenue is tough to deal with. Joe understands and says he will stay in touch, and keep trying.

Joe flies back to Seattle on the same plane he flew over on, what a surprise it makes sense. When he steps into the terminal he is grabbed by Joni, she is holding him tight saying she has missed him so much. Joe at first is embarrassed by Joni's enthusiasm but then decides, oh well what the hell, and picks her up hugging her back. He has missed her too, and tells her that. The others offer their hands to Joe welcoming him home.

CHAPTER 69

The Prince Albert arrives in Seattle after a hard two months, the crew are ready for some R and R and are jubilant except for Cookie. He has nowhere to go and doesn't know what he will do with himself. Captain Murphy invites him to come home with him, but Cookie tells him no thanks. Cookie doesn't want to be a bother, and will just wait around until the ship sails again. The ship ties up at the company dock and when Cookie walks off the ship he is met by three deputies from Georgia. They say they have a warrant for his arrest. Cookie nearly leaps into the water thinking it may be better to drown than face the law. Captain Murphy intervenes, he steps between the cops and Cookie. He demands,

"this man works for me, what right do you have arresting him for anything?"

The deputies aren't impressed by this loud-mouthed Irish bastard and draw their guns. Captain Murphy knows danger when he sees it and steps back. Cookie is worried for his friend and offers himself. The cops read Cookie his rights and of course Cookie agrees. Cookie thinks to himself, well at least I got the bad guys and that hell hole of a court house. He feels some satisfaction in that.

Captain Murphy arrives in Roses office and Carmen listens to his reports and is typing while she is listening. She is alarmed to hear about Cookie's arrest, and calls Rose over. She is angry and demands to know where is Cookie now?

Cookie is cuffed and taken to the airport, there is a small plane waiting there to take him to Georgia. Cookie has given up, he knows he is guilty; however, he isn't so dumb that he says anything. He hasn't said a word to anyone about anything. Cookie's only words were,

"I want a lawyer, it's my right."

The three deputies are big men and aren't gentle with the old man. Cookie is strapped in and the three flow in around him, he is surrounded by very big nasty cops.

Murphy tells Rose and Carmen about Cookie being hauled off by those Georgia cops. Rose always gets involved; she wants to know why? Jones has just returned with the Jet Ranger landing on the roof after delivering more parts to a ship. He has been flying for hours and is really tired. He finds the women gathered by Carmen's desk with Captain Murphy. Captain Murphy holds out his hand, and wanting to say hello to Jones. Captain Murphy has never forgotten Jones's time on his ship. Captain,

"well Mr. Jones, I see you still haven't learned to salute your betters."

Jones,

"I thought I told you that you can be replaced once."

Murphy,

"well now, so you did, but I'm still here, don't you know."

Rose draws them in to the problem concerning Cookie. Rose,

"Captain Murphy, has Cookie been working out for you?"

Murphy tells her that Cookie is the very best cook they have ever had, and we want him back. Rose tells him oh that's good, I like that man, he seems to be humble. Murphy tells her that Cookie is liked by all the men, and he has never had such wonderful meals ever. Murphy pats his rounded belly affectionately. Rose smiles at that, and goes on,

"it seems that Cookie was in a little trouble back in Georgia. She asks,

"wasn't Cookie at the camp that got burned down or something?"

Jones, says well he was the one that saved John-John from the KKK mob in the clearing in the woods. Rose remembers now and asks,

"do you think that has anything to do with what's happening now?"

Jones thinks it probably does; we need to get some really good lawyers who know about Georgia law. Rose asks,

"are there any?"

Jones doesn't know, he tells Rose about a civil rights lawyer practicing in Omaha who is by far the best. She is interested asking if that lawyer can practice in Georgia? Jones doesn't know, but if she likes he will ask and maybe Cookie's case is a federal case

Braidy comes whistling in yet again and even Jack groans. Braidy just can't carry a tune even if he uses a big dump truck. He goes into the kitchen followed closely by Jack. Braidy has been watching his dog friend and finds food that's less fattening for Jack. Jack doesn't like the healthy food much but downs it anyway. Braidy comes out of the kitchen with a roast beef on rye with let is tomatoes cheese and loads of mustard on board. Carmen asks,

"say Braidy could I have about all of the sandwich?"

"nope, get your own shrimp."

"Carmen growls at him and throws a rolled-up doughnut wrapper at him, and to her surprise it lands right on his plate. Braidy looks at her in surprise not saying a word. Everyone else looks at the plate than at Carmen and grins. Carmen wants to know what's the matter. Rose says,

"well dear, you just scored two points, you landed your ball in the middle of Brady's giant sandwich. Carmen is surprised too, but says,
"

"well certainly, of course, that's what I was aiming at don't you know."

Murphy takes it all in saying,

"so, this is why I can't get any service from this office, you guys are playing games all the time."

Rose consults with the company lawyers and they tell her that it would be very difficult for any of them to practice in Georgia. Rose wonders what the hell good are they, why does she pay them so much for so little. The lawyers suggest that she contact a Georgia lawyer who is licensed to practice there. Rose hangs up and turns to Jones,

"so, Jonesy about this Omaha lawyer, can you contact him?"

Jones,

"yes of course, I will call her and ask if she is available and if she can practice law in Georgia."

Rose is saying oh ho, so she's a woman, one of your early conquest no doubt. Jones, tells Rose that was just a passing thing nothing there. Rose says,

"they're had better not be anything more than that, anyway please do what you can for Cookie." Jones says,

"ok but you need to conference in with me, first because you're the boss and also its self-defense for me. Rose and Jones go over to Carmen's desk where the landlines are and Jones asks Carmen to look up a name for him. Carmen,

"what, do you think, I'm just the operator here?"

Jones tells her no way baby, you're the one that is in charge of knowing everything he doesn't. Carmen wonders at that one, does that make sense? She finds the number for the law firm where Jolene works. The law firm has grown in the past 25 years and is easy to find. Jones has to leave a message for Jolene, she is in court. After 2 hours Jolene calls back,

"hey Jonesy, how the hell are you your old bum you."

Jones grins at that and Rose growls like Jack. Jones wipes the grin off and continues,

"The reason we're calling is because we have a man who needs defending. He is from Georgia and works on one of our ships as a cook. Rose introduces herself and explains further to Jolene of the conditions and alleged charges as she knows them, Jolene,

"Georgia is a difficult state to practice law there is a lot of prejudice attitudes still. I can practice law anywhere in some cases, for instance if there is some sort of ADA violation."

Jones, remembers a conversation with Cookie long ago while they drank coffee at the little kitchen table. He remembers that Cookie admitted to him that his mother was a black woman. Cookie said that down south he could pass for white. The sun is so bright that most people just get darker because of the sun. Jones tells her that Cookie is half or at least part black having a mother who was a black woman. Jolene says that can help, it doesn't matter what the reason actually is, almost anyone can be discriminated against for almost any reason. Jones is asking her if she would be willing to look at Cookies case?

Jolene says she will if she could have a few days to finish some cases she is working on. Jones tells her of course, they just jailed him this morning. Jolene wants contact information that has Cookies location and she needs permission to represent Cookie. Rose says she will retain Jolene as Cookie's lawyer. Jolene agrees and Rose offers Jolene a $5000 retainer. Jolene says that's too much, and Rose explains that that is the usual amount. Jolene just loves these discrimination cases; she believes in the ADA laws and all other laws that can help people who are beet up by the system and society.

Jones tells Rose,

"see that wasn't so bad, aren't you glad I know the right people?"

Rose taps his cheek in warning, he is treading on thin ice she says.

CHAPTER 70

Barbra is wanting to spend more time with Braidy, she fishes almost every day and has a large group of clients. She is fun and usually can provide the guys with good fishing. She has helped the villagers with their plumbing. The outhouses have been replaced with indoor bathrooms. Barbra asks for advice from Roses maintenance people, she asked them to show her what needed to be done. Barbra has done much of the work herself and Braidy has done his best. He isn't much of a plumber but he can help. She uses something called Pex Pipe and SharkBite fittings to connect the plumbing. They have dug lines mostly by hand, and created a waste pond for the sewage. The pond isn't the nicest thing to smell on certain mornings when the wind is out of the east but will be better when the bushes grow tall enough to hide the pond. The village people aren't plumbers either but you don't have to be a plumber to dig a ditch. Barbra hired a company to dig a well, the equipment had to be brought over from the mainland on a barge. Rose donated tug boat time to move the barge. The well was dug in one day and fresh clean water is now available for the village people. The villagers use the water only when they need to, they start a generator once or twice a day as needed. The dairy barn is easier to keep cleaner with running water. Most people have learned to use water when the barn is being cleaned up after milking

    Barbra has done well with her village people, she has help them to improve their quality of life and their hygiene is better too. Barbra uses rain water that has been trapped in a cistern for bathing and cleaning and buys bottled water for drinking. Braidy usually brings a case of water when he comes for visits. Braidy flies his float plane each time he visits Barbra and ties it at the dock. She can hear him coming and he always buzzes her house to let her know he has arrived.

Barbra has been getting headaches daily and they are becoming intense. Braidy sees her rubbing her head and asks,

"what's the matter baby?"

Barbra,

"oh Mr. Braidy sir, my head it is hurting too much, and I am not seeing with eyes so much either."

Braidy asks,

"how long has this been going on?"

Barbra,

"oh, it's nothing, just a little headache don't you know."

Braidy watches her more closely and notices that she misses the doorway in her house, she glances off the edge of the doorway. Barbra thinks nothing of it, but Braidy is concerned she can't fly with vision like that. Braidy goes up behind her and wraps his long arms around from behind. He tells her that he will take her to the doctor in the morning. She tells him no I don't want no doctor. Braidy turns her around and he can see that she is afraid. For this woman to be afraid of anything is unusual He takes her in his strong arms gently and says,

"don't worry my Barbra, I will take care of you."

Barbra is crying against his chest, this is a new experience for Braidy, but he doesn't care, he loves this woman and will do everything he can for her.

The medical news for Barbra is no good, she has a tumor in her head. The tumor is not benign and will cause trouble. Braidy is uncertain what to do, he has never loved anyone like Barbra and turns to his friends. Braidy,

"what do I do if she dies, how do I get along without her?"

Rose gathers her favorite uncle into her arms and tells him that she loves him. Braidy isn't even hungry and sits on the floor under the windows where Jack and Carmen use to sit when they were troubled. Jones knows trouble and goes over with Carmen, they sit on the floor beside him and Jack knowing he is needed comes too.

Barbra and Braidy have an appointment with a leading Cancer Doctor. The woman is around 50 years young and is compassionate and understanding. She is soft spoken and treats them gently. She tells Barbra that her disease is very bad, she will need surgery followed by very aggressive chemo therapy and maybe radiation. The prognoses aren't favorable, she wants to be up front with her. Barbra is brave, she knows that everyone can die. Barbra is sad because she wants to spend more time with Braidy. Braidy isn't as brave and tears leak from his big brown eyes. He isn't ashamed of tears for Barbra, and says,

"doctor, I'm not a rich man but I have enough. Anything she needs please do."

The doctors name is Jessie, and she wants to help this very special couple. She says if they are willing to go to another country for treatment there is a procedure she has been following. Barbra looks up at that, and says,

"Ms. Doctor, I am from Jamaica don't you know, I never got to be an American citizen, not yet." Dr. Jessie provides them with contact information to a clinic in Costa Rica, and Braidy is suddenly hopeful. They tell Dr. Jessie they want to try talking to the people in the clinic in Costa Rica

Dr. Jessie,

"please understand that the clinic will help maybe with managing the pain that will get worse, and it's only for a short time. You will need some strong pain killer."

Braidy is devastated, how can he think, and he wants to grab Barbra and run away from all the trouble they have. Barbra is more up beet; she says she has lived a good life even though she is only45 now. Braidy needs his people around him and tells Barbra that he wants to let the people at work know about her. Barbra,

"oh now Mr. Braidy sir, don't you be feeling so bad, we got a little time and we have good times already, don't you worry, you'll find someone prettier than me that's for sure."

Braidy thanks Dr. Jessie and takes Barbra's hand, they walk out feeling like entirely different people. Braidy needs to talk to Jones, and the others, he knows they will be with him so that he can help Barbra.

Braidy takes Barbra back to the island, she needs to be alone some. He will come back to her after visiting with Rose. Braidy will barrow Barbra's boat and when he returns will spend the night with her. She asks him if he could bring her some strawberries please. Braidy will do anything for her and kisses her and is off. When he arrives at the headquarters building, he takes the private elevator to the office. Rose and Carmen are together at Carmen's desk, they are talking to Jolene from Omaha about Cookie's case. Rose looks up and exclaims,

"oh, Braidy what's wrong?"

She knows this man so well she knows there's something very wrong. She gets up and moves over to him and wraps her arms around him. She doesn't say anything, knowing that when he is ready, he will tell her. Carmen comes and holds him too. Braidy in a small voice says,

"Barbra is dying, she has only a few months, she has a brain tumor, there's no cure for her."

The two women are crying now and Braidy is numb. Jack comes over softly quietly and stands near. Braidy holds Rose and Carmen in a group hug and when Jones comes in from flying, he can tell there's something wrong. He walks over to Jack and lays his hand on Jacks head. Braidy sighs and begins to speak,

"she has been having headaches more and more often lately and finally it got so bad she was having problems with her vision.

He tells them that they went to a specialist who ordered tests and the results are clear, the tumor is large and has wrapped all around her brain. She will suffer more pain as the disease progresses, that's what Dr. Jessie told us. Barbra wants to be alone for a while on the island. I will go back there soon; she wants me to bring her strawberries. Rose, wipes her eyes on her sleeve and says,

"oh, Braidy were so sad for you and Barbra, of course you will tell us if there's anything you need? Braidy,

"Barbra has family in Jamaica and I need to ask her what she wants to do about telling them. She doesn't talk much about home any more, I think this has become her home now. Rose tells him that anything he needs or wants to please ask them and they will help. Jack comes over and nuzzles Brady's hand, not licking just being close to his friend. Braidy stoops down and pets Jacks big head and ruffles his ears. Jack leans closer to Braidy and wines in sympathy

CHAPTER 71

Braidy takes Barbra's boat back to her island with the strawberries and after tying up the boat slowly walks over the lawn and onto the porch. Braidy feels it before he sees it, Barbra is gone. He finds a long letter written in her very expressive hand, and knows she has made it easier for him. She writes,

"my darling Mr. Braidy sir, I am gone now, I won't tell you how or where, just know that I am asleep in my ocean, and at piece. I have left you everything, and you will find my will with this letter. Please know my love, that you are the only man that I have ever truly loved, and I will miss you and love you for always. Please Mr. Braidy sir, don't cry for me, I'm ok, I just couldn't make life more difficult for you, please live your life, find someone new for me. I will always love and miss you but you must go one, so my love, Goodbye, be well."

Braidy is stunned, he had no idea she would end her life so that he wouldn't be inconvenienced, he sobs with sadness for his woman. Braidy sits with her letter in his hand for hours, finally he lifts his teary face and can't see a thing. He has been there for so long it is dark. Braidy, doesn't feel anything even though it is cold now. He gets up and looks over the lawn to the sea, the moon is nearly full and he can see waves breaking. Braidy sighs and thinks she is right, life goes on, but without Barbra, he wonders how or why. Braidy can't stay here alone without Barbra and unties her boat, well now his boat, for whatever that's worth. He uses her GPS to get himself to shore and remembers his satellite phone and calls Jones,

"hey Jones, it's me Braidy, could you come and get me at the boat dock you know where we tie up the boats?"

"hey Braidy yes of course, are you alright?"

"I don't know if I'll ever be alright, I just need a ride for now."

Rose sees Jones's look and comes over close to listen in, she knows by Jones's face that something more is bad. Jack gets up from his corner and moves over to be with the family. Jones tells him that they are on their way, just wait there, it will be ok. Braidy says he will wait where he is and hangs up. Jones tells Rose what Braidy has asked for and she and Jones go with Jack to the basement garage. Rose is crying again, she does that so easily some times, and Jack pokes his head between the front seats to get closer to her. Rose says,

"I think Barbra has died sooner than everyone thought she might. Jones,

"yes, I feel that too, we will bring Braidy home with us, and will stay with him until he is ok"

Rose simply tells him thank you.

They find Braidy just standing a tall figure looking lost and forlorn. Rose gets out and runs to him, she pulls him into her and holds him tight. Braidy just stands there just looking so sad. Jack and Jones come over to and surround him. Jones coaxes him into the car and Jack climbs in beside him in the back seat. Jones and Rose get in the front, then Rose changes her mind and climbs in the back beside Braidy. Rose takes his hand and Jack is close on the other side and Jones drives them back to the headquarters building

CHAPTER 72

Cookie is so alone, he isn't hungry at all, he is in a cell with lots of other guys, he isn't surprised that most are black men. That Rose has sent some sort of lawyer to talk with him and she is kind. They talk in a small room close to the pod. She is slim and smells like flowers, and touches his hand or shoulder often. She is reassuring and confident, and tells him that she will represent him in court. She says that Rose from the shipping company has hired her to defend him but Jones is the man she knows best. Cookie,

"do you think anyone can hear me here? And Well you see; I did blow up the court house."

Jolene doesn't like hearing that, although she will do her very best to defend this man, it's her job weather he is guilty or not. She looks around too like Cookie, and then decides that no one is listening. For one thing, the jail is at least 75 years old like the court house was and there are no listening devices Jolene doesn't take any notes, the prosecutor hasn't provided her with any discovery. So far all they have is a statement from a Mable Williams saying that she knew Cookie and after the explosion he disappeared. Jolene knows that being accused of a crime is enough for the prosecutor to issue an arrest warrant. She tells Cookie she will motion the court to have the case dismissed for lack of evidence, the court will deny of course. She then will demand a bail hearing She says she will get to work for him, and does he need anything? Cookie asks her for Roses address please, he wants to thank her for helping. Jolene thinks that's nice of Cookie and gives it to him. Now, is there anything else? Cookie tells her no thank you, and I really appreciate you coming to see me. Jolene tells Cookie she'll be back, and she hopes to have him out soon.

Jolene motions the court for Cookie's bail hearing and it is set for the next morning. Jolene stays in a flee trap hotel, not the Hilton that's for sure. She finds the diner where Cookie met Mable and finds a booth. Jolene recognizes Mable right away from Cookie's description. The restaurant isn't busy and she orders a salad and coffee. When Mable brings out her order Jolene asks her if she has a minute? Mable recognizes a good listener, and asks if she can sit down? Jolene,

"Yes of course, I want to ask you some questions about Cookie, he's being accused of blowing the court house up. Will you tell me what you know about Cookie?"

Jolene doesn't mind and asks how is Cookie and can she visit him? Jolene tells Mable that hopefully Cookie will be out on bond in the morning. Mable is glad and claps her hands together. Another customer comes in, he is a truck driver with a big belly, he sits on a stool at the counter. When Mable gets his order, she comes back to Jolene. Jolene continues,

"Do you know if Cookie had any explosives in his room? Mable,

"Well you see, I was never in his room; he was or should I say is a private man, he liked his privacy, all he left me was his bird."

Joleen asks Mable questions that mean nothing, just trying to get a handle on the situation. Mable's says,

"Oh dear, you haven't touched a bite, aren't you hungry? Jolene leaves her a very generous tip and waves a cheery good bye.

In the morning, Jolene is in a library conference room where a judge from another district allows Jolene to practice law in the state of Georgia but only for Cookie's case. Joleen,

"Thank you Your Honor, if it pleases the court, we are requesting a bail amount to be set for my client. Your Honor, if it also pleases the court, would it be too soon to request a decision on the status of the charges against my client, I have no discovery, what is my client charged with exactly?"

The Judge, "Mam, you surely must know of the destruction of the court house with pertinent records needed in this case and many others, the court needs some time."

"Yes, Your Honor, in the meantime, I motion the court to release my client on his own recognizance?" Prosecutor jumping up knocking a large stack of papers on the floor,

"Objection objection, this is a very serious crime, and this man is guilty."

Jolene,

"Your Honor, I object after all it is constitutional, the accused are innocent until or unless proven to be guilty, the prosecutor can't even produce one shred of evidence."

The Judge, wipes his forehead it's not hot, and says,

"She's right, you have no discovery, you need something besides a missing person report that turns out not to be true. Mr. Meyers, do you plan on leaving the state?" Mr. Meyers, that is Cookie's name, answers, he would like to go back to Washington if possible, Mr. Prosecutor,

"your Honor, "Prosecution objects, Mr. Meyers could board a ship and go off to who knows where, we may never find him again."

Joleen says,

"If my client is innocent than why does it matter where he is?"

Judge holds up his very white hand and says,

"Wait, I have a letter here from Rose Martin president and owner of Big Lift Shipping and Lumber company guaranteeing Mr. Meyers location and will produce him when requested. Ms. Martin owned the logging camp where so many workers were killed and it has been proven that poison was used causing most deaths. The records are in Atlanta and are intact. I release Mr. Meyers on his own recognizance pending further procedures. And Mr. Prosecutor, if you don't have any more evidence then this nonsense then I will throw this case out of my court room, is that clear?"

Prosecutor,

"Your Honor, you know we have missing files because of the court house explosion."

Judge,

"Times are tough all over, even still the law is the law, no evidence no case that's the law in this court room, now good day to you sir."

CHAPTER 73

Braidy flies with Jones in the float plane, they know that the big boat is missing probably Barbra used it last. Jones is flying and Braidy is telling him about Barbra. Jones is a good listener and says yes or no at the right places. He can't say for sure what Braidy is talking about, it doesn't matter, Braidy needs to talk it out. Jones flies in a search pattern not even realizing that he was until Braidy tells him. They find Barbra's fishing boat just drifting with the tide, it's the location of the shark attacks. Jones shudders to think of what must have happened to Barbra. Braidy wants to land and Jones brings them in stopping near the boat. Braidy climbs out on a float and onto the boat. Jones gives his friend some time just waiting, when Braidy turns to him Jones comes over too. Braidy,

"My Barbra was a brave woman, she used her father's revolver to end her life, she stood on the pulpit here pulled the trigger and fell in the water."

Jones sees that the revolver is tied to a rail with some cord and Braidy has pulled it out of the water. There are no bullets in any chambers, only the empty cartridge, only one shot needed. There's nothing left of Barbra except what's here. Jones takes his friends arm and talks quietly. Jones says,

"Your right my friend, she was a very brave woman, she didn't want to be any bother, it takes a lot of love and care to do that for someone else. She really truly loved you man, you'll be ok, I'm here to help, anything at all and it's yours."

Braidy says,

"Do you think this boat will stay here with the anchors down?"

Jones knowing his friend says yes it will, and helps Braidy back to the plane. They will come back later for the boat or maybe the village people will help.

CHAPTER 74

Jones drives them back to headquarters building, and Rose Carmen Jack, Nancy and Joni are waiting for them. Rose invites everyone up to the roof, she has a nice fire going in the grill and offers dogs, potatoes salad and cold beer. There are soft drinks for shrimps and teetotalers she knows it's too early for Braidy to feel better of course but she thought some food might help. The dogs are a variety of meats, all prepared by the Italian meat market. Roes is celebrating the release of Cookie; she says that that Jolene is really good. Jones says he knows, she got him out of a pickle a few times. Rose says,

"oh yes, this is the first I've ever heard of that Mr. Jones."

Jones waves it off tipping an ice-cold beer to his lips, it was nothing. Braidy sits with Jack, they share his fluffy bed, its large enough for two. Jack sticks by Braidy the entire time, he knows his friend is hurting and provides Jack like love like only Jack can. Joni is there too, she doesn't eat much, she wants sweet things more and more, she loves chocolate, snickers bars are her favorites. Jones,

"So, what's next for Cookie?"

Rose filling a plate for herself answers,

"He can come back here if he wants, I had to practically sign my life away guaranteeing his return upon their request or should I say demand. Jolene says that if there isn't any substantial evidence theirs no case."

Jones swallowing a delicious bite of Polish dog,

" That's' the law I've heard."

Rose offers all around dogs in Round the Corner buns with any toppings people want. They munch down dogs and scoop up potato salad, and Braidy and Jack share a dog.

CHAPTER 75

Braidy is surrounded by his friends, his family now, and he will be ok. Joe is off again in China and Joni is less worried this time. She has been helping Braidy get over Barbra's death. Jones and Rose are helping each other with the growing company and Jack is still hungry.

THE END

www.ingramcontent.com/pod-product-compliance
Lightning Source LLC
Chambersburg PA
CBHW030321100526
44592CB00010B/519